Born Fundamentalist, Born Again Catholic

David B. Currie

Born Fundamentalist, Born Again Catholic

IGNATIUS PRESS   SAN FRANCISCO

Cover art: *Delivery of the Keys*, by Pietro Perugino
Sistine Chapel, Vatican Palace, Vatican State
Scala/Art Resource, New York

Cover design by Riz Boncan Marsella

© 1996 Ignatius Press, San Francisco
All rights reserved
ISBN 0–89870–569–x
Library of Congress catalogue number 95–79976
Printed in the United States of America ∞

To my wife,

Colleen,

a companion par excellence

Contents

Preface

By its very nature, this is a personal story. I started writing it with no intention of letting strangers read it. Its original purpose was to explain my spiritual pilgrimage to my children. I knew that, as they matured, they would be approached by evangelicals attempting to persuade them to leave the Catholic Church. While I was writing, I decided to share my story with a few evangelical friends as well. I hoped to answer some of their questions. Before I started to circulate it to non-Catholics, however, I had four Catholic friends read it over to check it for any inadvertent heresy. After all, I am a new Catholic.

One of those friends is a priest. He suggested that this story might be helpful to others looking for a deeper relationship with Christ. There are already many explanations of fundamentalism and evangelicalism that Catholics can understand. There are very few treatments of Catholicism written in language that fundamentalists and evangelicals can appreciate.

I am by nature a rather private person, so I hesitated. I was finally convinced by a few paragraphs on generosity in *Furrow*, by Josemaría Escrivá: "Self-giving is the first step along the road of . . . union with God. . . . If you make an effort, with the grace of God that is enough. Put your own interests to one side, you will serve others for God. . . . The more generous you are for God, the happier you will be." I felt that perhaps I needed to be generous enough with my privacy to share my experiences with whomever they might help. It is in that spirit that I have agreed to "bare my soul".

This story was not intended to embarrass anyone or to anger anyone. It merely relates the reasons for my family's pilgrimage from fundamentalist Christianity to the ancient Church that Christ founded, the Catholic Church. To paraphrase the Apostle Paul: when I started this journey through life I was a fundamentalist of fundamentalists (cf. Phil 3:4–6).

This story should be read in order. Although the first three sections are not the longest, they are the most important. Later sections will not make sense without the background supplied in the first three sections. I have written about all the issues as I worked through them in my pilgrimage.

The reason behind my writing should not be forgotten. My intention was to explain my decision to people who had shared my former religious milieu: fundamentalism and evangelicalism. Because of this, I decided to use the New International Version of the Bible. Some of my friends still prefer the King James Version, but most now accept the NIV. I do not think any of the points discussed are substantially changed by using a different translation. Paraphrases, however, can be misleading.

I have generally used evangelical ways of speaking because it was for fundamentalists and evangelicals that my explanations were intended. Catholics may find one of these ways of speaking annoying. I have not used the title "saint". For example, Catholics would generally speak of "Saint Paul". Evangelicals generally call the Apostle Paul merely "Paul". That may sound much too familiar and disrespectful to many Catholics. For better or worse, I have decided to use evangelical ways of speaking.

Perhaps the most important reason I consented to publish this personal account has to do with my own indebtedness to certain other authors. I have read the life stories of Christians my whole life. It was the truth I encountered in their stories that stuck with me over the years. Eventually, the truth all accumulated in my head, fell into place, and made sense. If my experiences help even one other Christian on the pilgrimage of life, then it is enough.

There are those who say that people do not care about the truth anymore. I don't believe it. Religious commitment of any sort is too much work if one does not believe it truly answers life's deepest longings. Our relationship with God is rooted in the way things really are, or it is nonsense. Granted that all of us merely "know in part" (1 Cor 13:12), but people change religious affiliations because they are convinced that the change brings them closer to God and his truth. Most people do not change merely because of warm fuzzy feelings. A loving social group can make the transition easier, but it is not the primary cause behind the transition itself.

The combination of truth and commitment, over time, is practically impossible to resist. That is the appeal of the martyrs. They had the truth and were committed enough to die for it. The truth, firmly believed, can "set your soul on fire". If nothing else, people will come out of curiosity to watch you "burn". This is the story of my inner burning for a closer relationship with Christ—and of where the Truth led me.

Acknowledgments

I would like to thank the many people who encouraged me in this endeavor. Among them are Father Peter, Daniel, Mark, Sandra, David, Virginia, and, most of all, Colleen and our children.

I agree wholeheartedly with John of the Cross: "Should I misunderstand or be mistaken on some point, whether I deduce it from Scripture or not, I will not be intending to deviate from the true meaning of Sacred Scripture or from the doctrine of our Holy Mother the Catholic Church. Should there be some mistake, I submit entirely to the Church, or even to anyone who judges more competently about the matter than I."

I

The Beginning

I have vivid memories of the day President John F. Kennedy was shot. A sixth-grader, I was playing on the playground when the rumors started. Just before the dismissal bell at the end of the day, the principal made the announcement over the PA system. JFK had been assassinated. School was dismissed in eery silence. Tears welled up in my eyes as I walked the half mile home that afternoon. My sorrow was almost overwhelming for a sixth-grader, not only because our President was dead, but because in my heart of hearts I knew that he was in hell. He was a Catholic, and I was a Christian fundamentalist.

I was the second child in a family of four children, the only boy. When I was a small child, I was lucky enough to have my mother at home full time. What a great time we had! My family was, and still is, very close.

My parents met at Houghton College after my mother transferred there from Nyack Bible Institute in New York. They returned to Chicago and were married by A. W. Tozer, their pastor and the author of several Christian classics, including *The Knowledge of the Holy*. I was born while my father was attending Dallas Theological Seminary. At various times each of my parents taught at Moody Bible Institute.

Because my father was a fundamentalist preacher, I was a "P.K." (preacher's kid). I have fond memories of sitting in church every Sunday, listening to my father preach. Through him I had an education in theology before I ever attended Bible School. We children went to church for about six services each week. We always sat in the fourth row. An older man always sat in the fifth row. He would signal us with a cough and then pass us coconut candies under the pew. We would reach under our seats and then try to unwrap the candy quietly, so no one would hear.

Our church celebrated only Christmas and Easter. I had never even heard of a "church calendar" that recognized any other events of the Incarnation. We did celebrate the secular holidays, such as Mother's Day. My grandfather was born in Scotland and came to the United States as a child, but he never failed to celebrate Orange Day.

Every day, after dinner, our family read a passage from Scripture, sang a hymn, and prayed together. I heard virtually nothing of the Christians who lived between the end of the first century and the eighteenth century. D. L. Moody and Hudson Taylor were two of my more contemporary heroes, but most of my heroes were from the Bible. Ever since I can remember, I diligently tithed 10 to 20 percent of my income to support dozens of Christian works, such as Awana, Campus Crusade, Child Evangelism Fellowship, Jews for Jesus, Pacific Garden Mission, Wycliffe Bible Translators, and Youth for Christ.

We were called fundamentalists because we believed in the fundamentals of the faith that had been formulated in reaction to the rise of modernism in American Protestant theology around the beginning of the twentieth century. We still accepted the twin pillars of the Reformation, *sola scriptura* (the Bible alone is our final authority) and *sola fide* (we are justified by faith alone). In addition, we thought it important for our churches to teach clearly the Deity and Virgin Birth of Christ, the inspiration and inerrancy of the Bible, the substitutionary atonement accomplished by the crucifixion, and the literal Resurrection and still future but imminent Second Coming of Christ to set up his Kingdom (premillennialism).

One became a Christian by believing that Christ died to pay the penalty of sin, by admitting that all one's own efforts at heaven were useless, and by accepting Christ as one's personal Savior. This was the prerequisite of any "personal relationship" with God.

On a practical level, being fundamentalist meant keeping myself separate from the evils of the world and from the errors of liberal Christianity. And so I did not dance, attend movie theaters or the ballet, use tobacco, drink any sort of alcohol, swear, play cards, gamble, or date non-fundamentalists. (Our Southern counterparts accepted the use of tobacco but forbade mixed swimming.) It may sound rather strict, but it did keep me out of trouble. I was almost thirty when I first stepped into a tavern. I was impressed by the free peanuts available with my Pepsi. When I took my own children to see old Walt Disney reruns like *Bambi*, I too was seeing the movies for the first time.

It made it easier that the adults around me lived up to the same standards. I never detected in my parents any of the hypocrisy that the major media try to portray within fundamentalism. I never heard my parents swear, even if they hit their thumb with a hammer. I had no doubt that my parents were following the truth of God in the best way they knew. They taught me that commitment to the truth is always worth the effort, regardless of the sacrifice.

As I was growing up, I had the privilege of seeing the

leadership of the fundamentalist movement up close. Theology professors were frequent guests. I can remember sitting at dinner in my parents' home and asking theological questions of the presidents of seminaries and the founders of evangelical mission agencies. I found these men to be Christians of the highest character, intense and earnest in their commitment to God.

I was taught to be polite and neighborly to Catholics and other people we considered to be non-Christians, but always with the motive of someday seeing them become true believers, as we fundamentalists were. I was taught how to turn a friendly conversation into one in which I could share the gospel. When I was in a social situation and failed to accomplish this, I sometimes felt a twinge of remorse or even guilt.

My whole life revolved around the church and its people. Very few of us had friendships outside our fundamentalist faith. In high school I had a crush on a girl who taught Sunday School at a Methodist church. I knew I could never date her.

Our worldview divided the world into neat categories. Fundamentalists were the true Christians, like those of the first-century Church. We were taught that those who questioned the fundamentals of the faith were liberals, a group that included most non-fundamentalist Protestants. Liberals might make it to heaven, but it was rather unlikely.

It was bad to be a liberal, but it was much worse to be a Roman Catholic. Catholics were not even really Christians because they did not understand that salvation is by faith alone. Catholics were going to hell because they tried to earn their salvation by good works rather than by trusting fully and completely in the finished work of Christ on the Cross. No one was good enough to *earn* salvation. We could prove that from the Bible. As a result, most of our converts were Catholics.

The last of our categories was made up of those people who were total unbelievers. There weren't many of them in our neighborhood during my childhood. I met my first atheist during my junior year in high school.

Our view of history explained much of this. The Church had been pure and true to her original charter for the first three hundred years of her history, until Emperor Constantine supposedly made it advantageous to be a Christian in the Roman Empire. Then the Church's teachings became polluted with error, and her membership began to be filled with nominal Christians—in other words, Catholics. We were convinced that many of the Catholic practices and beliefs were man-made traditions invented in the Dark Ages to control people through fear and superstition.

All through history, we believed, God had preserved a remnant of people who had protected the truth just as we fundamentalists were doing now. It was easy to see that the Roman Catholic Church did not contain these believers. All one had to do was to look at their beliefs. Did Catholics ever read their Bible? We did, every day. So much of what Catholics believed, we thought, was in direct opposition to God's word. I had never actually read any Catholic theology for myself, but, nonetheless, I was sure that I knew what Catholics believed. We seldom pondered the many areas of agreement we had with Catholics, such as the Deity of Christ, the Virgin Birth, and the inspiration of Scripture.

In particular, two beliefs of Catholics bothered me. The first was their amillennialism. Catholics believe that we are presently in Christ's Kingdom, so there will be no literal one-thousand-year reign of Christ in the future. Fundamentalists believe that the Kingdom is yet to come, only after the rapture and a great tribulation. The rapture was that moment when Christ would snatch his followers off the earth so that God's judgment could descend on the unbelievers left on earth—the tribulation. The rapture might happen at any moment. In fact, many fundamentalists seemed surprised that it had not already occurred. We knew we lived in the "end times" because we believed Scripture indicates that the tribulation would start within one generation of the Jews' return to the land of Israel in 1948. I can remember as a child becoming extremely frightened if I could not find my mother at home after school. It was always possible that I had "been left behind" and would have to suffer through the tribulation alone.

The second belief of Catholics that was a problem for me was the insistence that Mary remained a virgin after Christ's birth. This and amillennialism seemed to contradict the obvious meaning of certain Scripture passages. I knew the Bible was without error. If the Catholic Church disagreed with the Bible, the Church had to be in error.

There were other beliefs I found offensive as well: purgatory, prayers to saints, veneration of images and relics, the Assumption, the Immaculate Conception, elevation of Mary to co-redemptrix and mediatrix, indulgences, salvation by works, the daily re-crucifixion of Christ in the Mass, regeneration by baptism, belittling of scriptural authority, infallibility of the pope, the insertion of the Apocrypha into the Bible, adoration of the Host, addressing priests as "father", and confession of sins to men rather than to God. Catholic practices with regard to images and relics really distressed me. Whenever I saw a statue of Mary, I thought of Catholic idolatry.

What made things even worse in the fundamentalist view was a perceived lack of commitment. It seemed to us that

Catholics did not really believe anything strongly enough to stand up and be counted. When we were in high school, we were the only ones in gym class who refused to square dance. We refused because we believed dancing was wrong, but we found it extremely difficult to put up with the undesired attention of our peers over this matter. (I had to pass out towels in the locker room during the six-week session on square dancing.) We knew, however, that if Jesus wanted us to abstain in front of fifty of our peers, he would give us the strength to endure any embarrassment. Why were there no Catholics willing to take the heat for their beliefs as well?

Looking back on my experiences now, I recognize that the fundamentalist environment I grew up in was very anti-Catholic. I plead guilty to having had a stereotypical WASP superiority complex. Harvard professor Arthur Schlesinger, Sr., could easily have had me in mind when he said that prejudice against the Catholic Church is "the deepest bias in the history of the American people".

On Sunday evenings at our church we had testimony times from the congregation. People would stand up and tell the rest of the assembly what God was doing in their lives. When I heard the testimonies of some of the people, detailing how God had saved them from the Roman Church, I remember thinking I was really lucky that I had not been born a Catholic.

In Bible studies, the "right interpretation" of a passage was often contrasted to the Catholic view. Catholic jokes were not uncommon in our circles. We laughed about the "bells and smells" of High Church worship. Some fundamentalists called Catholics "mackerel snappers". I knew several people who called the tail of the roasted chicken the "pope's nose". I started to use the term as a child without ever recognizing how offensive it was or what it implied about papal teaching.

These were things that never happened, however, in the company of Catholics. Our Catholic acquaintances would have been shocked at how we talked of their beliefs in their absence.

It was not that we hated Catholic people, because we didn't. We believed, however, that the structure and teachings of the Roman Catholic Church were a false religion, only marginally connected with original Christianity. We saw fundamentalism as the true Christianity. Catholics were spiritually lost, and we had to help them find Christ without being polluted ourselves. They needed to be saved. So we had contests in Sunday School to see who could invite the most "unsaved" kids to church.

I can still remember making the decision as a child to place my faith in Christ for my own personal salvation. I struggled with the "assurance of my salvation" until I was a teenager. At fourteen, after a public profession of my faith in Christ, I was baptized. (Christians of our convictions would *never* baptize an infant.) From that point on, I never had any doubt that God was working in my life. I knew that I had been "born again".

Ever since I can remember, I knew that I wanted to utilize my talents for God. I had been taught that, if the God of the universe was directing me to do something, I had better obey or face the consequences of my rebellion. Studying the Bible was the only fail-safe way of knowing God's will. As a teenager, I memorized verses and even whole books of the Bible. As a child, I had been able to think of nothing more holy than entering full-time Christian service, so that was my intention.

I had friends who attended Bob Jones University, Wheaton College, Columbia Bible College, Biola, Prairie

Bible Institute, Moody Bible Institute, or Grand Rapids School of Bible and Music. I attended Bible school after high school graduation, transferred in order to complete my degree in philosophy at Trinity College (now Trinity International University) in Deerfield, Illinois, and entered full-time ministry in Chicago. I had been scheduled to start at Dallas Theological Seminary, but because of my commitments in Chicago I entered Trinity Evangelical Divinity School (TEDS) in the Masters of Divinity program instead.

During my education there, I stopped calling myself a fundamentalist. The reason was not that I specifically disagreed with the doctrinal content of fundamentalist beliefs. I just grew increasingly uncomfortable with the fundamentalists' strident tone. How could it be squared with the scriptural command to love one another?

The only major difference between fundamentalists and many evangelicals centered on "separation": how involved we should be with unbelievers and liberals. If there is one distinguishing characteristic of fundamentalism, it is this issue of separation. I had been raised a "second-degree" separationist.

"First-degree" separationists would not fellowship with Christians who had compromised with error, including liberals and Catholics. Being "second degree" meant we did not fellowship even with Christians with whom we *did* agree if *they* fellowshiped with those with whom we did not agree. For example, second-degree separationists did not cooperate with the Billy Graham Crusades, because Billy Graham included liberal clergy in his program. Increasingly, as I studied the Bible, I found fundamentalist teaching concerning separation impossible to justify.

Like so many of my generation and the next, I started to call myself an evangelical. This meant that I had entered into a personal relationship with God through Christ, that my theology was orthodox (not modernist), and that my lifestyle was committed and evangelistic. However, I cannot say that I ceased being a fundamentalist. I still firmly believed all the "fundamentals of the faith". With the exception of one profitable four-year period in a Presbyterian church, I continued to be active in the same type of fundamentalist churches I had attended before this name change.

When I speak of evangelicals, I am referring to the group of which I was a part, the intellectual descendants of the Anabaptists.

At the time of the Reformation there were two very different groups of Protestants. The Lutherans, Calvinists, and others rejected only those doctrines of the Catholic Church that they believed directly contradicted Scripture. Everything else remained. Anabaptists, on the other hand, rejected all doctrines of the Catholic Church that they could not directly support from Scripture. This was much more radical. The changes were far more extensive.

As believers in this more radical branch of Protestantism, we were sure that the Bible was the only reliable source for doctrine, that premillennialism was essential to the proper understanding of the church, and that the church should be free from the state (hence the name "free churches"). Wheaton College, Trinity Evangelical Divinity School (TEDS), Dallas Seminary, Moody Bible Institute, Biola, Talbot Seminary, and many other institutions all required their professors to toe the line on these issues. These evangelicals fill the pulpits and pews of many types of churches—Baptist churches, Community churches, Bible churches, and Evangelical churches. Theologically, there is no crucial difference between most of them and most fundamentalists.

I am fully aware there are other types of evangelicals within such denominations as the Lutheran, Presbyterian, and Methodist. I am not implying that these other types are not truly evangelical. But if I had been raised as one of them, my journey would have been quite different. Catholics ask me how they can distinguish between these two groups of evangelicals. An issue that is probably the easiest to use to explain the difference is infant baptism. There are occasional exceptions, but as a rule the "mainline" evangelicals accept infant baptism, and the "free church" evangelicals, to which I belonged, do not.

The "free church" evangelicals and fundamentalists are more like each other in most theological issues than are the two sorts of evangelicals. Perhaps two illustrations will be helpful. When my father attended Dallas Theological Seminary, the majority of students called themselves "fundamentalists". Many students now at Dallas feel more comfortable with the label "evangelical". Yet the theology taught at Dallas has not changed appreciably in all those years. Second, I remember meeting an evangelical Baptist a few years ago whose testimony involved being "saved out of the Presbyterian Church". Although his language was a bit too abrasive for some, that general feeling pervades the "free" evangelical churches. They have the same misgivings about "mainline" evangelicals that fundamentalists have.

When I use the term "evangelical", most of the time it would be accurate to substitute for it the word "fundamentalist". But the same does not always hold true for the term "mainline evangelical". To help distinguish between these two groups of evangelicals, from this point on I will capitalize "Evangelical" when referring to these "free" Evangelicals. By this usage, the word "Evangelical" is a subset of the more inclusive word "evangelical".

While at Trinity, I met and married Colleen. At the time I

proposed, she was a Christian Education major at Wheaton College, planning on becoming a foreign missionary. In her I found a woman who was my complement. She too was totally committed to God's will. We married when I was twenty-three.

I took about three years of Greek at Trinity. I came to love and respect my professor. He could be ruthless in his pursuit of what the text actually said. God help the student in his class who was sloppy in exegesis. That approach reinforced the direction of my earlier upbringing. The truth mattered.

I found that biblical theology appealed to me more than systematic theology. It seemed to me that all the systematic theology I read had areas in which the truth of a certain passage had been "fudged" in order to make the system as a whole coherent. Almost unconsciously, I started to keep a mental list of verses that could not be explained by any evangelical system I could find. I figured that one day those verses would fall into place somehow.

At Trinity my philosophy professor introduced me to C. S. Lewis' writings. I devoured all that I could find. At the time, I thought Lewis was a bit hung up on ritual (sacramentalism), but I overlooked this fault because of his brilliant reasonableness. Reading him strengthened my faith. Through his writings I later encountered some of his heroes and friends —George MacDonald, G. K. Chesterton, and J. R. R. Tolkien.

Another discovery I made during my education was that I enjoyed business and that I had a talent for it. In the process of this discovery, I met and was helped by some truly remarkable people. For the first time I made friends with Catholics. Then a time came when I knew that God wanted me out of full-time Christian service. Once I became sure of it, I wasted no time in leaving. My earlier taste of the business world eventually resulted in my starting my own business when I was thirty-three.

As an adult, I have served in full-time Christian service and as a trustee, deacon, elder, evangelism trainer, choir director, and Sunday School teacher for adults. I have been a member of the boards of two para-church ministries. Colleen and I have moved a number of times since being married and so have been involved in several different evangelical churches. I have been satisfied with the church experience that my family and I have had. Nothing is ever perfect where people are concerned, but all the churches of which we have been members deserve at least a "B" on any report card. I would give the church we just left an "A" without any second thoughts.

Perhaps because of my background, my friends and extended family were appalled when I decided to become a Catholic. Hadn't I been too well trained in theology to fall for the errors of Catholicism? Why did I make this decision at the rather late age of forty? It was not easy. I wrestled for years with the issues. My parents and two of my three siblings are devoting their lives to full-time Christian ministry. I have many friends involved in bringing Catholics "to Christ". I knew that I would most likely lose friends and the support of my extended family.

I wasn't even sure if Colleen would join me in my new faith. We had discussed much of my thinking, but could I ask her to endanger a lifetime of friendships by making this change? Would I drive a wedge between my children and myself that could never be removed or overcome? (My eldest was thirteen at the time.) They had been taught in youth group that their Catholic friends needed Christ (in other words, they were not truly Christians). My family always was and still is my most precious possession on earth. Why was I being compelled to make this change?

As an Evangelical, I was convinced that truth was objective and knowable. If something was true for one person, then it was absolutely true for all. Truth had an objective character, not merely a subjective one. In his books Francis Schaeffer called this "true truth". Now I found the truth breaking into my thinking with such effectiveness that I would never be the same. At the time, I *did not want* to be a Catholic, but eventually I felt I had to in order to keep my intellectual integrity.

I had visited various Catholic churches but had always viewed the experience as similar to visiting a museum: it was an interesting place but lifeless. Now I visited a Catholic church with a different purpose. I tried to picture myself worshipping God in such surroundings. My mind revolted. The experience was like a kick in the stomach. The church seemed much too beautiful, the statues too numerous, and the atmosphere too other-worldly (and yet so intensely physical) for me.

The thought of actually attending a church like that for regular worship gave me a knot deep down in my abdomen. I was used to simplicity, if not austerity, in my worship surroundings. The church of my childhood did not even display a cross anywhere. A verse popular among Evangelicals says that God must be worshipped "in spirit and in truth" (Jn 4:24). We harbored a strong anti-physical bias that was challenged by everything in that Catholic church.

My first time ever at Mass came after Colleen and I had decided to join the Catholic Church. It was a disconcerting experience. Everything was so hard to follow and to understand. The music was unfamiliar, and few people sang along. The Lord's Prayer was truncated. With the continual standing, sitting, and kneeling, I felt out of place in church for the first time in my life. The order of the missal was totally incomprehensible to me. The experience certainly did not make the decision to change more attractive to me. It frightened me to the very core of my being.

Yet I had to make this change to Catholicism anyway. Truth was calling me. When I had finished writing my letter of resignation to our Baptist church, I sat down in our living room and wept like a child. After proofreading the letter, Colleen sat on my lap and mixed her tears with mine. That night I told good friends of our decision to become Catholic and that I was not happy about it. I found it easy to relate my feelings to those of C. S. Lewis when, at his conversion to Christianity, he said he was the unhappiest Christian in all of England. Once I had become convinced that the Catholic Church really was Christ's Church, however, at no point did I doubt that I would join her. If I had discovered a pearl of great price, I knew I would sell all I had to buy it (Mt 13:44–46).

Earlier, when I had first told my wife and then later the children, they were sceptical. Colleen said that she would love me even if I became a Muslim but not to expect her to get excited about my decision. (How could I help but love a woman this loyal?)

I decided to slow down my own pilgrimage in an attempt to give the rest of the family time to catch up. For years, every night after dinner we had read the Bible and prayed together as a family. Now, after dinner, we discussed each of the important issues as a family. When I couldn't find an answer, my eldest would jokingly ask me to call "Dan the Answer Man". Dan was a new Catholic friend whose grasp of theology was nothing short of breathtaking. (I am eternally in the debt of Kimberly Hahn for introducing me to Dan.) We had great family fun during our investigation. Colleen started to get excited when she, too, saw the truth drawing me to Catholicism.

After six months of talking, studying, reading, and praying together, I can joyfully say that my entire immediate family became enthusiastic about our new commitment to the ancient Church of Christ, called Catholic. Colleen and I received our First Communion together on the Second Sunday of Advent. Our family lit the Advent wreath and carried the bread and wine forward. After introducing Colleen, our six children, and myself to the congregation, I spoke for a few minutes. Halfway through, I started to choke with emotion. Our parish priest, the physical embodiment of gentle charity, put his hand on my shoulder, and I was able to finish. This is what I said:

> I am about to recite the Apostles' Creed. As you know, this is a customary way of announcing the desire to become a part of this church as members. I was raised a Protestant, and I studied in a Protestant seminary. I have always believed in this Creed, but only within the last year have I become convinced that the Catholic Church is the Church of which this Creed speaks. I know that to many of you that fact has always been self-evident, but it was a decision I came to only after tremendous research and battles of the soul at the rather late age of forty-one. I accept all the teaching of the Church as my own, but the major doctrine that has drawn me here is the Church's teaching concerning the Real Presence of Christ in the Eucharist. That doctrine is central—life-changing, mind-stretching, soul-strengthening—but most of all, true.
>
> Today my wife and I celebrate our First Communion with you as Catholics, and I proclaim with my whole heart, soul, and mind,
>
> > I believe in God, the Father almighty, Creator of
> > heaven and earth;
> > and in Jesus Christ, his only Son, our Lord:

Who was conceived by the Holy Spirit, born of the
    Virgin Mary, suffered under Pontius Pilate, was
    crucified, died, and was buried.
He descended into hell;
the third day he arose again from the dead.
He ascended into heaven and sits at the right hand of
    God, the Father almighty;
from thence he shall come to judge the living and the
    dead.
I believe in the Holy Spirit,
the holy Catholic Church,
the communion of saints,
the forgiveness of sins,
the resurrection of the body,
and life everlasting.
Amen.

The congregation broke into applause, and I knew I had
come home. Like so many others, I have found the Catholic
Church to be everything my heart had longed for from my
earliest memories. The joy of my salvation has been renewed
in a truly remarkable way. Not since childhood have I
whistled and sung this consistently throughout the day. I find
it more true the longer I am here: I was "born again" as a child
to worship with this Church. I would have vehemently denied it at the time, but I was "born again" a Catholic. Since
that childhood experience with God, I had been on the hunt
for truth. Now I had found it in a totally unexpected place:
the Catholic Church. If I had been left to my own desires, I
could not have designed worship any better. Of course, that
makes sense when I consider who did design the worship of
this Church.

All our children were baptized Catholic shortly after the
Advent season. Our eldest was confirmed along with Colleen

and me just before the Easter season. I chose James as my patron saint because his epistle means so much to me.

What drew us to the Church? One of my pastors thought I must be looking for a social group with a less demanding moral code. He should have known better. The Catholic Church is more stringent on moral issues than any non-Catholic church. The Evangelical church has relaxed its moral standards in the last three generations as a result of societal pressures and yet does not even seem to be willing to admit it. There are Catholics (even priests) who do not successfully live the Church's teaching, but only the Catholic Church has had the fortitude to "stick to her guns" on all moral issues. Not so long ago all Christians, including Evangelicals, opposed divorce and remarriage, birth control, homosexuality, masturbation, euthanasia, abortion, and so forth. (I was at Trinity when abortion was legalized in the early 1970s. The overwhelming response by students and faculty was "So what?" Only with the help of Catholics were the few notable Evangelical exceptions able to prod us out of our indifference.) The Catholic Church's refusal to alter the original Christian position on these and other issues has caused some to leave the Church and some to try to change the Church, but absolutely no one joins the Catholic Church looking for moral laxity.

What drew us? A relative accused me of wanting to rebel against my upbringing and my family. There was one minor problem with this notion. I asked that relative to point out anything in the first forty years of my life that had been done out of rebellion. No answer. I went to the Bible school, college, and seminary that my parents recommended. I brought my girlfriends home so my family could meet them and give me their advice. Even now, I am still exceedingly thankful for the moral consistency and the loyalty to scriptural teaching that were modeled for me in my childhood by my family. I have done dumb things, thoughtless things, and selfish things. I am an independent and strong-minded person, but I have never knowingly rebelled against anything for which my family stands. Add to that the fact that the Catholic Church is not a place conducive to rebellion. If rebellion had been my objective, the Unitarian Church, or no church at all, would have fit the bill much better.

What drew us? A friend said I must be entering a mid-life crisis. I even read a book about that, at his suggestion. Although anyone could find interesting things in the book, I felt then and now that it did not provide the answer so far as I was concerned. I was not looking for a new god but answering the call of the same God I had always known. The real question was: Would I obey him wherever he led me in search of the truth, even if the fullness of that truth was to be found only in the one church Evangelicals reject as inherently flawed?

One pastor friend pointed out, "*No one* does what you are contemplating! It's unheard of!" I had to admit I had never heard of anyone else leaving Evangelicalism for Catholicism. Talk about feeling isolated! (Since then, I have encountered a small army of us.)

What drew us? Another pastor (our church had three full-time and two part-time pastors) felt we must be unhappy with something at the church to think of changing. Actually, the reverse was true. I was fulfilled in my ministry as a deacon and Sunday School teacher for adult classes. The first quarter I taught the class, we grew from around twelve adults the first Sunday to almost fifty on the last Sunday. We had friends. Our children were enthusiastic about our church and its youth group. I felt the church had recently made some important, correct choices for the deacon board. I was upbeat about its future.

It is very interesting to me that Evangelical friends immediately concluded that something emotional had drawn me and my family to Catholicism. We would try to discuss issues of truth and error, and they would want to discuss "anything but". Everyone was so very sure we were falling into spiritual error, and yet no one was willing to discuss the issues objectively. One friend from TEDS, now pastor of a large Evangelical church, told me, "If you are willing to go through what is about to happen to you just for the sake of 'truth', then you care about truth a lot more than I ever have." I came to the conclusion that it would have been much easier for Evangelicals to handle our decision if there had been an ulterior motive on my part. It would have been even easier for them if I had just decided that the beauty of the Catholic church building and service was something that I wanted to experience. That was not the case.

I cannot help thinking that if most Evangelicals could just get past their initial emotions on this issue, they also would follow the truth wherever it led them. As unusual as this may sound to any Evangelical who has not investigated Catholicism directly and carefully, I see my decision as a natural outgrowth of my Evangelical commitment. Evangelicals have eighty percent of the truth, including most of the important issues. I found that eighty percent, plus the missing twenty percent, in a careful examination of the Catholic Church. (Let me hasten to add that no single person's *understanding* of the truth measures up to one hundred percent.)

A TEDS graduate and his wife who asked us for the reasons behind our decision are an excellent example of others who came to the same conclusion. They are solid, educated Evangelicals. To our amazement, God was working independently in their lives, and they ended up joining us in Catholicism.

What drew us? Primarily, it was the study of Scripture. Scripture? Yes, the Bible drew us into Catholicism. There were other books and people and influences, but just as the study of the Bible had earlier moved me from fundamentalism to Evangelicalism, I now found it moving me to Catholicism. We became convinced through Scripture that the Catholic Church really is the Church that Christ founded, and for this reason she deserves our loyalty and support.

This firm conviction is the only thing on earth that could have enticed me to endure the suffering this decision has cost us. When I tell Catholics that Colleen and I both lost some of our close friends over this decision, that people from our old Evangelical church avoid us when they see us in a store, or that some of our relatives no longer want to talk to one or the other of us, they look at us in disbelief. But it is true. Colleen once jokingly compared our experience to being in the Federal Witness Protection Program, which totally uproots you and gives you a new identity. We might as well have moved to another planet.

The explanation is simple, though not easy to accept. The Catholic Church views Evangelicals as fellow Christians who agree with her on 80 percent of the issues. The Church unequivocally teaches that we are all 100 percent Christian brothers. On the other hand, most Evangelicals believe that they possess the essence of the truth of Christianity. They believe that the Catholic Church's teaching concerning salvation is fundamentally and fatally flawed. From their perspective, the only Catholics who might actually be Christians are those who do not fully accept the teachings of the Church. In their view, an "informed Catholic Christian" is an oxymoron.

There is plenty of evidence of this Evangelical conviction. Almost all Evangelical churches rebaptize Catholics who convert to Protestantism. It is done thousands of times a year, in Evangelical churches all across America. (My mindset was such that I was surprised to learn that the Catholic Church accepted my fundamentalist baptism and would not even consider rebaptism as an option. I was accepted as a brother who had been a Christian since childhood.)

Evangelicals also spend tremendous amounts of money in Catholic countries to convert Catholics to Evangelicalism. I have had friends who are missionaries to such Catholic countries as France, Spain, the Philippines, Mexico, Honduras, and Colombia. When some Evangelical friends speak of the Christian church in Israel, they refer to it as being less than fifty years old. If I mention the Orthodox and Catholic Churches, which can be traced to the time of Christ in such places as Bethlehem, they dismiss them as nominal.

In our pilgrimage toward Catholicism, there were several intellectual threads in the process of recognizing that the truth demanded our reconciliation with Catholicism. Some of these threads were discovered later than others. Most of them overlapped in time. In the end, we found the threads had joined together to make a rope in our hands, pulling us irresistibly closer to Christ and his ancient Church. Rather than deal with all the issues in a strictly chronological way, I will attempt to review each one from beginning to end before moving to the next.

By its very nature, this is a personal recounting of my own thought process that led me to the Catholic Church rather than an in-depth theological treatise. At the end, I will list a few good sources with which any reader so inclined might start a similar investigation.

II

Communion and the Real Presence

Since my childhood, I remember sitting in a communion service once a month and hearing the words "This is my body" and "This is my blood." What exactly did Jesus mean by these words spoken the night before his crucifixion? He knew that his words were to be repeated throughout the entire world for the rest of time. Surely he put a tremendous amount of thought into how he would express himself during this crucial night. If Jesus had meant to teach Lutheranism, he could have said in a clear way "This bread contains my body." If he had meant to teach Evangelicalism, he could have said in a clear way "This bread only represents my body." But he didn't say either. Yet he was clear. In the clearest way he could say it, he said, "This *is* my body" (Mt 26:26–28).

A year earlier, Jesus had fed five thousand people with a handful of food. He had then preached a sermon that drove many of his disciples away. The sermon is hard to interpret in isolation, but it makes complete sense when understood in the context of the Last Supper. I had never linked the two until hearing the author Scott Hahn. He pointed out how important the timing of this sermon is. It occurred near Passover, one year before the Last Supper (which occurred on

Passover). A year later, the apostles would naturally remember and associate this sermon with the Last Supper, in much the same way that we reminisce each Thanksgiving about what has happened at past Thanksgivings. Actions and traditions at present Thanksgivings are enriched by the words and traditions of past Thanksgivings.

It is one of the longer sermons of Jesus recorded by the Gospel writers. It is obviously very important. Since relatively few Evangelicals are familiar with what this text actually says, I will quote all of Jesus' recorded words here, omitting the words not spoken by him. (It still might be helpful to read the entire chapter.)

I tell you the truth, you are looking for me, not because you saw miraculous signs but because you ate the loaves and had your fill. Do not work for food that spoils, but for food that endures to eternal life, which the Son of Man will give you. On him God the Father has placed his seal of approval. . . . The work of God is this: to believe in the one he has sent. . . . I tell you the truth, it is not Moses who has given you the bread from heaven, but it is my Father who gives you the true bread from heaven. For the bread of God is he who comes down from heaven and gives life to the world. . . . I am the bread of life. He who comes to me will never go hungry, and he who believes in me will never be thirsty. But as I told you, you have seen me and still you do not believe. All that the Father gives me will come to me, and whoever comes to me I will never drive away. For I have come down from heaven not to do my will but to do the will of him who sent me. And this is the will of him who sent me, that I shall lose none of all that he has given me, but raise them up at the last day. For my Father's will is that everyone who looks to the Son and believes in him shall have eternal life, and I will raise him up at the last day. . . . Stop grumbling among yourselves. . . . No one can come to me unless the Father who sent me draws him, and I will raise him up at the last day. It is written in the Prophets: "They will all be taught by God." Everyone who listens to the Father and learns from him comes to me. No one has seen the Father except the one who is from God; only he has seen the Father. I tell you the truth, he who believes has everlasting life. I am the bread of life. Your forefathers ate the manna in the desert, yet they died. But here is the bread that comes down from heaven, which a man may eat and not die. I am the living bread that came down from heaven. If a man eats of this bread, he will live forever. This bread is my flesh, which I will give for the life of the world. . . . *I tell you the truth, unless you eat the flesh of the Son of Man and drink his blood, you have no life in you. Whoever eats my flesh and drinks my blood has eternal life, and I will raise him up at the last day. For my flesh is real food and my blood is real drink. Whoever eats my flesh and drinks my blood remains in me, and I in him. Just as the living Father sent me and I live because of the Father, so the one who feeds on me will live because of me. This is the bread that came down from heaven. Our forefathers ate manna and died, but he who feeds on this bread will live forever (Jn 6:26–59, emphasis added).*

Let's review the passage. First, Jesus defines what we must do ("work") for God: we must believe in Jesus. The Jews then ask for a sign from Jesus to prove he is worthy of belief. Jesus responds by claiming that he is "the bread of life". This is an analogy just like "I am the door" or "I am the vine." It could be understood in a multitude of ways, unless Jesus goes on to explain his analogy. He does exactly that: "This bread is my flesh, which I give for the life of the world." Jesus says the bread of life is his flesh. Lest we not understand whether he means "flesh" in a real, physical, touchable way, he tells us next that it is the same flesh that will be given up on the Cross! He goes on to say that this flesh must be eaten by his followers.

The analogy has been clearly explained. There is no doubt about its meaning. If the flesh we eat for eternal life is meant in only a "figurative way", or "spiritually speaking", then so is the flesh of the crucifixion! Jesus equates the two. Either they are both literal, or they are both figurative.

Evangelicals have never wavered in their insistence that Christ really physically died on the Cross. A theologian espousing a merely spiritual crucifixion or Resurrection would, by definition, no longer be an Evangelical. I can think of no way for Jesus to have affirmed more clearly that he would literally give us his flesh to eat for our salvation.

The liberal theologian escapes this difficulty by saying that this dialogue is not really the words of Jesus. Evangelicals reject that thesis for another set of reasons, not germane to the present discussion. What is interesting about the liberal point of view, however, is that it sees the dialogue in John 6 as clearly and unmistakably supporting the Catholic view of the Eucharist: that Christ is substantially present in the Eucharist and that partaking of his Body and Blood does benefit us spiritually. Because the sacramental meaning is so clear in the passage, some liberal Protestant theologians assume the passage is a later fabrication. They reject the Catholic view by rejecting the authenticity of this passage.

Jesus taught that in order for us to have eternal life we must "eat his flesh". He repeats this phrase, or its variations, six times. Four of the times, the Greek word used is very graphic; it can be translated "to chew". This word is never used symbolically anywhere in the New Testament, the Old Testament, the Septuagint, or even in ancient secular literature. There is no hint in the text itself of the faith–versus–action dichotomy that the Evangelical tries to introduce. Belief accompanies obedience in actually eating. Jesus makes it clear that the flesh is literal, as the body on the Cross was literal.

This is the only place in the Gospels where disciples of Jesus left him over a doctrinal issue. This is also the first time we hear of Judas doubting the wisdom of his master. There is a Church that accepts Jesus' teaching here as truth, but I knew it was not any of the Evangelical churches.

Catholics believe that Jesus is really present in the consecrated Host. This is the only way to explain adequately Paul's assumptions in 1 Corinthians 11:23–32: "Whoever eats the bread or drinks the cup of the Lord in an unworthy manner will be guilty of *sinning against the body and blood* of the Lord. A man ought to examine himself before he eats of the bread and drinks of the cup. For anyone who eats and drinks *without recognizing the body* of the Lord eats and drinks judgment on himself." How could one be "guilty" of the Body and Blood of Christ if the service is only a memorial? Granted, the service is done in remembrance. Evangelicals and Catholics agree on that. But Catholics teach that it is more than that. We must *recognize* (discern) the bread for what it truly is, "*the body of the Lord*", or be judged. How much clearer could Paul be than this? I could find no textual basis for the Evangelical teaching that communion is *only* a memorial.

Catholic theology teaches that the host (bread) is changed into the substance of Christ's Body by a miracle of God (the priest does not magically make the bread and wine into God by his own power, as some claim Catholics teach). The appearances of bread and wine remain with all their expected properties. This is a continuing miracle. Because these properties are retained, a person would still get drunk if he drank too much from the chalice at church.

This distinction between substance and appearance is a little difficult for Evangelicals to grasp. I helped my children understand it by reminding them of the old, retired star that Prince Caspian met in *The Voyage of the Dawn Treader* by C. S. Lewis. In that story, one of the books in the Narnia series, some English children travel to another reality and meet a star that looks just like an elderly man. The sceptical child among them declares that stars are exploding gases and denies that this man can be an actual star that once lit up the night sky. The star replies that Narnian reality is different from earth's reality, but even in our world a star is not essentially exploding gases. The gases are only the elements of which stars are made. What something *is* can be different from what it is *made* of. There is a distinction drawn in the story between substance and appearance that helps the modern mind to understand Catholic theology. (It is interesting that C. S. Lewis, the darling of American Evangelicals, is such a strong defender of the Eucharist, purgatory, and other Catholic dogmas that Evangelicals detest.)

Another example of this distinction may be helpful (although admittedly imperfect). We tell our children that although playing with matches *appears* to be harmless fun, in *reality* it is extremely dangerous. In advancing these explanations, however, I need to be clear. Catholics believe in the Eucharist, but *not* because of these analogies. We are simply using our reason to shed some small light on a truth that the Bible clearly teaches. We believe it because Jesus taught it.

The consecrated elements of the Eucharist are treated with utmost respect by Catholics because, in spite of appearances, there is the Real Presence of Christ in these elements. Jesus said it. Paul taught it. Never would the leftover elements be tossed into the garbage at the end of a Catholic Mass as is done in many Evangelical communion services. We treat them as we would treat God, because that is what they are in their real substance, although in appearance they do not differ from ordinary bread and wine.

Because Christ is physically present in the Eucharist, the church building is a special, holy place. For Evangelicals, worship in a gymnasium or forest preserve is just as acceptable as in any other place. For them, God is present *as spirit* anywhere they worship. For a Catholic, the physical presence of Christ is essential for corporate worship in the spiritual manner Christ intended. That can happen anywhere, but then that "anywhere" becomes holy because of Christ's real physical presence.

I used to think that the concept of the Real Presence of Christ in the Eucharist had been invented sometime during the Dark Ages as a ploy of the priesthood to gain power. Yet this truth is such a mystery that it seems unlikely anyone would invent it. Further, the most elementary reading of primary sources from the first three centuries of Christianity will show this theory of priestly invention to be the result of ignorance of almost unbelievable proportions.

In the early Church, everyone who wrote anything about the Eucharist believed in the Real Presence of Christ in the elements of Communion. Ignatius was the second bishop of Antioch and died a martyr at about the same time the Apostle John died. Speaking of the Docetist heretics, who denied the humanity of Jesus, he wrote, "They confess not the Eucharist to be the flesh of our Savior Jesus Christ, which suffered for our sins, and which the Father, of His goodness, raised up again" (Ignatius of Antioch, *Epistle of Ignatius to the Smyrnaeans*, 7). I thought that I had seen something new in John 6, until I noticed that Ignatius equated the flesh of the Eucharist with the flesh of the Cross, just as John had recorded Jesus as doing.

Irenaeus was a disciple of Polycarp who remembered

Polycarp's firsthand stories about the Apostle John. He used the Real Presence of Christ in the Eucharist to prove the resurrection of the Christian dead: "The Eucharist becomes the body of Christ" (Irenaeus, *Against Heresies*, 5.2.3). "How can they say that the flesh which is nourished with the body of the Lord and with his blood passes into corruption and partakes not of life?" (4.18.5). These texts, and many more like them, can be found in a Protestant translation, *The Ante Nicene Fathers*, published by Eerdmans.

I had always been taught that there was a "golden thread", or remnant of true Christians, who had always believed just as modern Evangelicals do now. Yet as I searched for anyone in the first three hundred years of the Church whose beliefs were even remotely related to Evangelical notions concerning the Lord's Supper, I came up empty. Christians were being persecuted and martyred during this period. Yet there is in existence a fair amount of literature from this time. Modern Evangelical theology, however, was nowhere to be found in it. The only way to accept the remnant theory is to accept it a priori, in spite of the facts.

For a full millennium of Christianity, there were no exceptions to this belief of the early Church in the Real Presence. It was the universal teaching of the entire Church. Not until Rationalism (and its firstborn child, scepticism) had started to transform the thinking of Europe would any movement call into question the Real Presence of Christ in the Eucharist.

As an Evangelical, I had heard the story exactly reversed. Superstition on this issue had not been added during the Middle Ages. Rather, truth originally transmitted by Jesus had been called into question by modern man. With Rationalism, something that could not be understood through reason was rejected. It has been said that mystery is an embarrassment to the modern mind. I have come to the conclusion that rejecting the reality of Christ in the Eucharist is merely a first step to denying other biblical teaching. Eventually, even the truth of the literal, bodily death and Resurrection of a historical Jesus is rejected. Protestant history certainly bears this out.

With the emergence of Rationalism and its attack on this doctrine, the Church convened a council that defined what all Christians had always believed about Communion since Christ had walked the dusty roads of Judea. This was the Second Lateran Council in A.D. 1215. Inasmuch as no movement in the first millennium of Christianity had seriously challenged faith in the Real Presence of Christ in the Eucharist, it had never been the subject of council debate, consensus, and decree. That the belief itself was universally accepted during that millennium is very easy to confirm.

Evangelicals profoundly misunderstand councils and their purpose. Just as with the first council, recorded in Acts 15, any council's purpose is to reexplore and reaffirm the original teaching of Christ that is presently being questioned. In Acts 15, the apostles did not make up new dogma but merely clarified the original deposit of faith concerning salvation by grace apart from the Old Covenant law. So it is with all councils. They reaffirm teaching that was given to the Church by the apostles but is currently under attack.

Protestantism is at its very core a child of Rationalism. The modern Evangelical asks, "How could Christ have held his own body in his hands at the Last Supper?" The Church Fathers wrote that this was impossible to understand rationally but that it was nonetheless true. It is a mystery. They gloried in the impossibility of it all. That the impossible is no problem for God can be seen just before Christ's sermon on the Eucharist, when he fed the five thousand. Modern sceptics, who are more consistent than Evangelicals, reject that miracle as well.

The Eucharist is central to worship in the Catholic Church. We believe that Christ (body, blood, soul, and divinity) comes to us and feeds our souls when we participate in Communion. On a practical level, the Evangelical has reduced the soul of man to little more than his intellect. As a result, Evangelical sermons tend to be from twenty to fifty minutes long every Sunday. That is how Evangelicals feed the souls of their faithful, through the mind. For them there is little way other than through the mind for the soul to be strengthened. For the Catholic, however, the will is the essential part of the soul. It is fed directly through its participation at the Mass. There is still the intellectual part of worship, but in the elements of the Eucharist, God can directly strengthen the Christian's soul against temptation.

Evangelicals may scoff, but as an adult who has lived the Christian life first without the sacraments and then with them, I can attest to the fact that they do work. My personality tends to be rather hard-driving. After we had been Catholics for about six months, Colleen told me that I had become much more peaceful and loving since becoming Catholic. I have no doubt that, if this is true, it is the result of being strengthened by the graces of the Church's sacraments.

After accepting the dogma of the Real Presence as truly biblical, my mind was put at ease about another problem, one I had not thought about for years. As a teen, I believed in the presence of a demon world. Witnessing for Christ on the beaches of America, we saw evidence of it. It always puzzled me that the worshippers of Satan in the sixties and seventies would parody the Mass when they worshipped. I could not understand why demons, who knew right doctrine but rejected obedience to it, should foster hatred of the Catholic

Mass if the Mass were merely a medieval superstition. If the Mass had not been instituted by Christ, then why would Satan worshippers make it the centerpiece of rebellion? Now I see that such a parody is a sure sign of rebellion against Christ precisely because the Mass *was* instituted by Christ at the Last Supper. Mockery of the Mass is mockery of its founder.

Catholic teaching on the Eucharist also helped me understand a passage in Zechariah that is unexplainable from an Evangelical perspective. "On that day... all who come *to sacrifice* will take some of the pots and cook in them" (Zech 14:20, 21).

This verse had been an enigma to me for sixteen years, ever since I had been a student at TEDS. I vividly remember standing in a hallway, in conversation with a man whose specialty was eschatology (future events as prophesied in Scripture). A young man approached us and asked the specialist about this verse from Zechariah. His question was, "If Jesus' sacrifice is final and complete, *why* will there be sacrifices needed in Jerusalem after the death and Resurrection of Jesus?" The scholar's face momentarily clouded with annoyance, and I have never forgotten his next statement. He admitted that he knew of no plausible Evangelical explanation for this passage.

The reason this verse is such a problem for Evangelicals is that virtually all of them agree that it speaks of events occurring in the Kingdom that Christ would come to establish (still in the future for Zechariah). But here is the problem. After Christ had died and set up his Kingdom, *why* would sacrifices still be performed in Israel? There is no good Evangelical response to that question.

Evangelicals are adamant that a priesthood here on earth is no longer needed; the need for sacrifices has ended. The crucifixion of Christ was the last sacrifice ever needed. But if the Evangelicals are correct on this issue of sacrifice, why would God reinstitute something superseded by the work of Calvary? Why perform sacrifices that are unnecessary?

Catholics believe that the Eucharist is a real, unbloody sacrifice that brings into the present time the saving effects of the once-for-all-time crucifixion of Jesus. The work of Christ on the Cross is finished. The crucifixion need never be repeated. But its benefits are applied to me in today's time-frame through the real sacrifice of the Eucharist.

The concept of making Christ's past sacrifice efficacious in the present is not foreign to Evangelicals. That is precisely what Evangelicals believe happens when a person puts his faith in Christ. One day Christ's work on the Cross has not yet benefited the person, and the next it has been applied through faith. Catholics believe their sacrifice of the Eucharist makes the grace of the Cross available today. Granted, it is a much more physical method.

I remember insisting, as an Evangelical, that sacrifices are no longer needed because of the Cross, yet I had no good explanation for Zechariah 14. I finally came to the conclusion that Zechariah had to be referring to the Eucharist. This is the only logical reason he would write that sacrifices will be done in the Kingdom after the Messiah's coming. When I saw the connection, I got so excited I ran into our living room and gave a "high five" to my thirteen-year-old son. The sacrifice of the Mass is being celebrated every day in Catholic churches, not only in Jerusalem but all over the world. The continuing sacrifices of the Church after Christ's death and Resurrection were foretold in the Old Testament.

I am amazed that Evangelicals totally miss the meaning of another important messianic prophecy. Karl Keating has pointed out in his book *Catholicism and Fundamentalism*: "The Lord has sworn and will not change his mind: 'You are a priest forever, in the order of Melchizedek'" (Ps 110:4). By definition, a priest offers a sacrifice. What did Melchizedek offer? Some Evangelicals are unaware of the fact that it was bread and wine that Melchizedek brought out to Abraham as an offering (Gen 14:18).

The next logical question is, "When did Jesus offer bread and wine as a sacrifice?" The only instance recorded in the Gospels is the Last Supper. Isn't it logical, then, that unless Evangelicals can point to another time Jesus fulfilled this function of the Melchizedekian priesthood, Jesus saw the Last Supper as the institution of a sacrifice? Otherwise the imagery of Psalm 110:4 is emptied of meaning.

This idea of Mass as sacrifice also explains best why 1 Corinthians 11:24–25 quotes Jesus as saying during the Last Supper, "This is my body, which is for you; do this in remembrance of me." As Scripture scholar Father Mitchell Pacwa, S.J., has pointed out, the Greek word for "remembrance" in this passage is a very technical word. Interestingly, it is also a relatively rare word in Scripture. Outside of its uses in the Last Supper, it is used only one other time in the New Testament. This is in Hebrews 10:3, where the remembrance is the act of *carrying out a sacrifice*. "Those sacrifices are an annual *reminder* [remembrance] of sins." If an Evangelical were to check his Greek Old Testament, he would find the word used only twice. Both times the remembrance is actually a sacrifice: "Put some pure incense as a *memorial . . . to be an offering*" (Lev 24:7) and "Sound the trumpets over your burnt *offerings* and fellowship *offerings*, and *they will be a memorial* for you" (Nb 10:10). (This word occurs two other times in the Old Testament—in the headings to Psalms 37 and 69. These were added later by commentators and so are obviously not actual Scripture, but they can indicate the meaning of the word Jesus used. Both speak of that Psalm as being used in conjunction with a memorial sacrifice. The Catholic Old Testament has one more occurrence, of a different nature, in Wisdom of Solomon 16:6.)

This Greek word "remembrance" is more than just "think about me by recalling this event to mind." It is a word fraught with sacrificial overtones, used in the Bible to mean "remind yourself of something by participating in a sacrifice." What a strange word for Jesus to use if he did not intend to set up the Eucharist as a sacrifice. In fact, Jesus' choice of this rather rare word is unexplainable if he did not view the Last Supper as a sacrifice.

I could no longer justify my Evangelical use of "remembrance" (or "memorial" in some translations) with a non-sacrificial meaning. While discussing the passages on the Eucharist, an Evangelical Bible teacher admitted to me that Evangelicals break almost all of their own hermeneutical rules (rules of interpreting the Bible) when they encounter these passages. Catholics are the ones with a consistent hermeneutical method.

The very core of Catholicism is the belief in the Real Presence of Christ in the sacrifice of the Eucharist. Pope John Paul II has said, "The Eucharist is the heart of the Church. Where eucharistic life flourishes, there the life of the Church will blossom." From the Catholic perspective, most other issues of discussion between Catholics and Protestants are peripheral.

I am not sure exactly how or when it occurred, but one day I knew that I firmly believed in the Real Presence of Christ in the Eucharist. After all, Scripture is so clear about it. Mark is the first Catholic I met who was enthusiastic about my pilgrimage to Catholicism. Mark said my belief in the Eucharist was simply a gift: the undeserved grace of God in my life. I wholeheartedly agree. When compared to all the other beliefs I have accepted all my life, such as the Virgin Birth, the Incarnation, and the Resurrection, I find it hard to justify the reluctance I felt for so many years to accepting what was clearly taught by Scripture and unanimously believed by the early Christians.

III

Scriptural Authority

On this subject of scriptural authority, let me begin by quoting from a letter I wrote to one of the pastors of the Baptist church we attended immediately before reconciling to Catholicism. The letter deals with the unresolvable problem of Protestantism: authority. It was one of several letters I wrote during the time I was leaving the board and then the church itself. My reading of the Old Testament that I mention in the second paragraph of the following extract was actually the first step in my pilgrimage to Catholicism. If not for this issue, I might still be an Evangelical with strong Catholic sympathies. The Eucharist showed me why I should be a Catholic. The Protestant problem with scriptural authority showed me why I could never remain a Protestant, Evangelical or no. The letter has been edited for its inclusion here.

> So that you better understand, let me explain the progression of my thinking to you. When I started this pilgrimage, I accepted the Protestant teaching of *sola scriptura*, or "only Scripture" (Scripture is the Christian's final authority for his faith).
>
> Several years ago I set a goal for myself of reading the entire Bible through in a year. I chose the NIV Bible because I had not done much reading in that version up to

that time. As I read the Old Testament, I was struck by several major issues. The most revolutionary for me was that I saw that no one could have established or maintained Judaism in the way God desired from the data found only in the Bible. There were too many holes and gaps: so much was assumed. I saw that a tremendous amount of what was involved in being a God-fearing, God-pleasing Israelite must have been passed down from generation to generation in an oral instruction (tradition). You want just one example? Try to reconstruct the process of offering a sin offering from the Old Testament alone. You can't get to first base! Reconstructing worship that would be pleasing to God from the Old Testament alone is impossible. There are many such examples.

This fact bothered me tremendously. It is hard for me to express in writing how unsettling the implications of that insight were to me. The God-ordained religion that Moses had helped to set up required the faithful transmission of oral tradition from generation to generation. Otherwise, the practice of Judaism in a way pleasing to God would have been impossible. I had always thought of the Jews as "people of the Book", yet the Book was not enough! This flew in the face of everything I had ever been taught. I knew it struck at the very heart of *sola scriptura* by illustrating the necessity of an authoritative oral tradition.

And yet, for us Christians in this age of grace, had not Jesus changed all that? Hadn't Jesus condemned all the traditions (binding oral tradition) of the Jews when he taught here on earth? The next step in my thinking came when I understood that the answer to that question is an emphatic "No." This was not my own insight; I encountered it in a verse that had been pointed out by Scott Hahn.

Jesus actually commanded the Jewish people of his day to obey the Pharisees' traditional teachings, orally transmitted: "The teachers of the law and the Pharisees sit in Moses' seat. So you must obey them and do everything they tell you" (Mt 23:2–3). But the seat of Moses itself is not to be found anywhere in the Old Testament! The seat of Moses was a product of that historic oral tradition so important to the Israelite faith. Jesus gives the authority of tradition his unqualified approval and commands his contemporaries to obey tradition's precepts. They are not given the option of obeying only those traditions they could justify with a "chapter and verse". Jesus explicitly includes "*everything they tell you*". Nor are there any "ifs, ands, or buts" to qualify the obligation to obey. The main problem Jesus had with the Pharisees is evidenced in the rest of the passage; they did not obey their own teaching. The authoritative nature of tradition is expressly taught here by Jesus himself.

We Evangelicals have always (rightly, I think) made a rather large point of the fact that Jesus gave his approval to the Old Testament books by quoting from them. We view that as his vote of confidence in their inspiration and canonicity. How could I have gone to Bible school, Christian college, and seminary without having this verse hit me between the eyes before? It establishes the fact that tradition (along with Scripture) had an absolutely valid right to my belief and obedience if I were living in the time of the Old Covenant. The Protestant dichotomy between truth found in Scripture and truth taught verbally by God's leaders through the generations had no place in Jesus' thinking.

How about the New Covenant? Did Jesus make the statement he did about tradition just for the benefit of the Jews hearing him (the Old Covenant was almost over, after all). Did the Holy Spirit inspire Matthew to record that statement of Jesus with no view of how the Church might interpret it? Or was Jesus stating something about tradition (remember, that is just God's truth passed down in oral form from generation to generation) that would set the stage for his greatest creation, the Church?

The fact that there was a tremendous amount of Jesus' life and teaching that was never written down cannot be denied. "Jesus did many other things as well. If every one of them were written down, I suppose that even the whole world would not have room for the books that would be written" (Jn 21:25). The writer of any given book of the New Testament chose, under inspiration, from the available data in order to fit the purpose of his letter or book.

Simply because something was not chosen for inclusion in a book did not mean it was no longer true, or that it was not actively taught by the apostles in the first century. In fact, in the case of epistles, the reverse would seem to be more plausible. Many of the most common and well-known practices and teachings of the early Church would be the least likely to be included in any of the writings of the early Church for the simple reason that they would be least likely to be misunderstood or called into question and thus require a written reinforcement or correction. This has been called the "occasional nature" of the New Testament.

I could not avoid the possibility that tradition was important and acceptable. I started to enumerate in my mind the Catholic traditions that Evangelicals unthinkingly accept, such as worship on Sunday and the canon of the New Testament. (There are even some unbiblical traditions of Evangelicals, such as the popular election of pastors, elders, and deacons.) But Scripture pushed me to go one giant step farther. I have now come to the firm conclusion that the New Testament clearly and positively teaches that we are under the obligation to obey the verbal teaching (tradition) of the Church, just as we are under the obligation to obey clear mandates of the inspired New Testament. Disobedience of the one is just as serious as disobedience of the other.

A Scripture verse may be in order: "So then, brothers, stand firm and hold to the teachings we passed on to you, whether by *word of mouth* or by letter" (2 Th 2:15). The verbal teaching by mouth (oral tradition) has an equal authority with the written teachings of Paul. This verse, even if it were the only one on this topic in the entire Bible (it is not), would mortally wound the Protestant view that Scripture is all we need to know of the will of God for our salvation.

Elsewhere Paul instructs Timothy to take this truth he has learned and find men capable of protecting it and passing it on (note the emphasis on the oral nature of this truth): "And the things you have *heard me say* in the presence of many witnesses entrust to reliable men who will also be qualified to teach others" (2 Tim 2:2). This is a natural extension of Jesus' command to "go and make disciples." Christianity is a living religion, protected and passed on by people, not paper. We are not to be *merely* people of the Book but the people of God. Nowhere does Paul imply that the written word is to be used against the verbal tradition or the men entrusted with its protection. It would take the Gnostic heretics to think up that strategy. It has been a plague on the Church ever since, starting with its use against the Apostle John himself.

The verse I always used to quote on the sufficiency of Scripture actually reinforces the Catholic view: "All Scripture is God-breathed and is useful for teaching, rebuking, correcting and training in righteousness" (2 Tim 3:16). The Bible is useful for all these, but this verse certainly never promotes Scripture as the final authority for our faith.

This is why I said what I said in my previous letter: "To

paraphrase Protestants, only those doctrines taught in the Bible are to be trusted for our theology. This very statement, however, is logically self-destructive! The simple fact is that (according to your own criteria) this statement cannot be trusted, because it is not taught in the Bible. The Protestant view of the Bible is unbiblical. Your view of Scripture is unscriptural." I have concluded that, concerning scriptural authority, the Bible clearly teaches the opposite of what the Protestants are trying to say it teaches.

If that makes you feel a bit queasy, then, believe me, I know how you feel. That is precisely the point at which I went into the library last spring, diligently (shall I say even frantically?) looking for a way out of this corner. Protestant theologians have no answer. If you don't believe me, spend some time looking for yourself. Read only Protestants. I did. You will find most of them don't even deal with the issue. Those who do will admit they have no good answer, but they take the Protestant view concerning Scripture by faith.

You mention the Trinity as an example of a doctrine we both ascribe to, yet it is not mentioned in the text of Scripture. For clarity's sake, we must distinguish between the *teaching* of Scripture and the mentioning of a specific theological *word* in Scripture. I believe the Bible does teach the substance of the Trinity, even though it does not use the word "Trinity". This issue of biblical authority apart from and above all other authority is an entirely different issue. The Protestants have used as the basis for their whole system of authority an idea that is not only not mentioned but not taught in the Bible—anywhere. If you think that it is, then show me. That is precisely what I have been asking the leadership of this church to do for several months.

In college I majored in philosophy. I remember the fascination I experienced when we studied the person who says, "I will accept as true only what science can experimentally validate as true." That person's worldview (rather common among Americans today) is self-destructive, because the statement itself cannot be validated by its own criterion. If you read the quotation again, you notice that it cannot be scientifically proven. The statement is outside the realm of science. Yet that is what the person is claiming to reject, all truth outside the realm of science. So the modern worshipper of science has accepted a logically invalid premise on which to base his beliefs. His system cannot be true, because its foundation is internally inconsistent. What he is really saying is, "I will accept as true only what science can experimentally validate as true —except for this one statement."

Another example of this error is the relativist hedonist who says, "There are no moral absolutes." The hedonist is in logical trouble because that very statement is a moral absolute. He is saying it is a moral absolute that there are no moral absolutes. His system self-destructs. It cannot be true regardless of how popular it is in America today. What he is really saying is "There are no moral absolutes . . . except for this one."

Another common example of this problem within the very root of a statement or system is the person who says, "All generalizations are false." This very statement is, of course, a generalization, and so the statement is nonsense. It self-destructs. He is really saying, "All generalizations are false—except for this one."

The Protestant is in exactly the same logically invalid position as are the people in these three examples. Nowhere does the Bible teach that Scripture is the sole authority for faith. Authoritative? Yes! Only Scripture? No! It is not only that the *word* is not used, as with the Trinity; it is that the very *concept* is unbiblical. The Protestant is really saying, "Only doctrines explicitly grounded in the

teaching of the Bible are ultimately trustworthy—except
for this one." The system cannot be true with an internal
inconsistency such as this.

The Bible does give us a way out: "the church of the
living God, the pillar and foundation of the truth" (1 Tim
3:15). Christ set up his Church, living from generation to
generation, to be the guardian of his truth. The Church is
the arbiter of what is true and what is not. It uses the Bible
and reverences it, but it must not place the Bible into a
position the Bible itself specifically rules out—that of being the only source of authority in a Christian's life.

The issue is not whether our view of the Bible is "high"
or "low" but whether our view of the Bible is biblical.
Unless you can show me how I am mistaken, I can only
point out the obvious: the Protestant view of Scripture is
unscriptural. If that conclusion is true, the whole system
of Protestantism, logically speaking, comes crashing down
upon its adherents, with eternal consequences.

Your friend and brother in Christ,
David B. Currie

P.S. I have not here dealt at all with how the earliest Christians viewed the issue of scriptural authority. What did
they teach regarding truth and where to find it? I will
quote only one early Father, but he is representative.
Ignatius was leader of the Church in Antioch, a martyr by
the act of Emperor Trajan. He wrote these words within
ten to fifteen years of the Apostle John's death (and so after
the New Testament canon was completely written): "The
bishop embodies the authority of God the Father, . . .
show him every mark of respect . . . defer to him" (*Epistle
of Ignatius to the Magnesians*, 3). And again: "It is proper for
you to act in agreement with the mind of the bishop;
. . . by your unity taking your keynote from God, you may
with one voice through Jesus Christ sing a song to the

Father. . . . It profits you, therefore, to continue in your flawless unity, that you may at all times have a share in God" (*Epistle of Ignatius to the Ephesians*, 4). Passages such as these are what prompted the statement in my previous letter: "For fifteen centuries the bishop was the final authority. Along came the Protestant reformers and set up a new authority."

The pastoral staff contacted me after receiving this letter and promised an answer. I waited months for an answer of any sort. I was surprised when it never came. My Catholic friends were not. They knew there was no answer.

To this day, when I tell people we were reconciled to the Catholic Church because we came to see she was the true Church of Christ, their responses are revealing. Catholics look at me as if to say, "Well, of course, didn't you always know that the Catholic Church was the real Church, even as a Protestant?" (No, I did not! If I had, then I would not have remained a Protestant!) Evangelicals usually respond with unbelief or anger. Occasionally, a better-educated Evangelical will give me a sad, knowing look and ask something along the line of "How is your walk with Christ doing?" ("Much better" is my most honest answer.) They know, but don't like to discuss, the Achilles' heel of Evangelical theology: a lack of divinely approved authority. Their system is man-made.

After making the transition to Catholicism, I remembered religious discussions I had had with an employee years before. Gerry was a good worker whose primary interest was his religion: the Worldwide Church of God, also known as "Armstrongism", after its founder. Sometimes, after work, we would go to a restaurant to discuss religion. He loved these talks. As I look back now, I know Gerry was trying to convert me.

His church did not accept the person of the Holy Spirit as equal with the Father. We discussed every Scripture passage that related to this subject. I could not convince him that it was a biblical concept. Although I knew his conclusions were wrong, I had to admit that his interpretation of each passage was reasonable. I ended up falling back on the Apostles' Creed and the Nicene Creed for clarification of Scripture. Gerry would not accept them as authoritative.

I now understand that Gerry was merely being more consistent with Evangelical assumptions than I was. He refused any authoritative input from sources outside the Bible, and he ended up without the person of the Holy Spirit. He thoroughly and consistently rejected oral tradition handed down from bishop to bishop. Evangelicals would agree that the result is a quasi-Christian cult.

While interacting with my peers in the late sixties and early seventies, I became aware of another area of silence in Scripture. All the institutions of our culture were under attack at that time, including marriage. I found that although it was easy to defend the permanence of the marriage bond from the Bible, it was not possible to define from Scripture alone just what constituted the beginning of a marriage. That knowledge was assumed by the biblical writers. In fact, the evidence pointed to the fact that the requirements for initiating a marriage changed throughout the history of the Bible. The Bible alone was insufficient for any serious defense of marriage. In the early seventies, that made for some awkward conversations.

As a twentieth-century businessman, I have been conditioned to distrust verbal promises and statements. Only something that is in writing can be "taken to the bank". This is a modern concept, however, not a Christian or biblical one. Jesus entrusted his gospel to people, who entrusted it to the next generation of people. The Holy Spirit can protect truth through people at least as well as through the written word, modern American prejudices notwithstanding.

Protestantism's unresolvable problem with authority forced my decision. In spite of my emotional loyalty to the faith in which I was raised, I could no longer remain a Protestant. Either I had to become a Catholic, or I had to settle for agnosticism. The latter has never had any appeal for me. I knew Jesus was real. I knew that his life and death were real and significant more assuredly than I knew that my own were. I took a month off from work to spend more time in concerted reading, thinking, and praying. I thank God that, at the end of that month, the Catholic Church was there when I was ready for her.

This was the watershed issue that changed the character of all of my subsequent thinking and research. But for this issue, I might have remained an Evangelical with tremendous admiration for the Catholic Church. This issue forced me to become a Catholic with a deep-seated affection for Evangelicals. My entire approach to the questions was altered. No longer was it appropriate to ask, "Where is such-and-such a doctrine taught in the Bible?" The proper question should always be, "Is such-and-such a doctrine in agreement with the original deposit of faith given the apostles, both written and oral?"

The Evangelical starts with the assumption that Scripture existed first and that tradition was slowly and incrementally added to it as time progressed. What I had reluctantly come to recognize was that the original deposit was given to the disciples years before Scripture was ever penned. The Church was founded on this truth from Christ. Some of this deposit was then written in Scripture, some was scrupulously passed from bishop to bishop as oral tradition, and some was later clarified as dogma by the agreement of the bishops in the councils of the Church.

These sources, of course, should be expected not to contradict each other. If the Church teaches something as true, it is justifiable to check that it is not contradicted by Scripture. But if the Church teaches something and the Bible is silent or ambiguous, that does not mean the teaching is any less truly a part of the original deposit of faith given the apostles. The focus of my thinking changed from what is *biblical* to what is *true*. The first is always contained in the second, but all of the second is not necessarily contained in the first.

When an Evangelical asks "Where is that doctrine in the Bible?", my response is usually "First show me from Scripture why you believe all Christian doctrines must be in the Bible." It can be frustrating for Evangelicals to confront this issue, but it is important for them to understand the lack of biblical basis for their question. Truth is at issue here.

IV

Authority

All Christians agree that we must submit to the authority of Christ, but where does that authority find its expression in the world today? One suggestion both friends and relatives made when we shared with them our plans to join the Catholic Church was: "Why not join the Anglican (or the Orthodox) Church? It would be so much easier for us to handle, and you could still feel as if you were joining the ancient Church." (Notice the emphasis on feeling.) As in almost every aspect of this pilgrimage, though, Scripture was important in convincing me that it was the Catholics who were right on the issue of authority.

After Jesus ascended into heaven, one of the first things the apostles did was to choose someone to replace Judas. Peter led the meeting and quoted two passages from Psalms to indicate that Judas' place must be filled: "May another take his place of leadership" (Acts 1:20). Matthias was chosen by lot. There is no record of any dissension or even discussion about whether this was a proper thing to do.

What can we learn from this? To me, it became obvious that the apostles understood that the leadership of the Church Christ was building through them was bigger than any one of them as individuals. Each occupied a "place of leadership", or office, that would continue after he was gone. Their responsibilities and privileges were not attached to them personally. Jesus had chosen them for service in his Church; but their office should and would be continued after their death. Evangelicals tend to overlook this important assumption of the apostles. Paul has this same assumption in a passage at which we have already looked: "And the things you have heard me say in the presence of many witnesses entrust to reliable men who will also be qualified to teach others" (2 Tim 2:2).

A careful study of the first recorded Church council—even the NIV Bible refers, in Acts 15:1-21, to the "Council of Jerusalem"—led me to interesting conclusions.

First, it is clear in the passage that, even before all of the apostles died, there was already a second generation of leaders exercising authority in the Church. These leaders are called elders, or bishops, and they are always identified separately from the apostles (Acts 15:2, 4, 6, 22). James is one of these leaders chosen by the apostles, though he was not one of the apostles (Acts 15:13). There were still other leaders, called "prophets", who were not considered to be bishops. Judas and Silas are two examples (Acts 15:22, 32). They were at the service of the bishops and apostles (Acts 15:22). When you add the office of deacon from elsewhere in the New Testament, it is not difficult to notice the top-down hierarchy already in place in the early Church.

On the occasion of the Council of Jerusalem, the bishops met with the apostles to determine whether the Mosaic law was necessary for salvation. To put the question another way: Were the Gentiles to obey the Bible or not? They decided that Gentiles did not need to be Jews first in order to qualify for God's grace. This meant that Gentiles were freed from obedience to much of what was contained in the Old Testament, the only Bible of that day. What is striking, however, is how the Council came to its decision. The Council did not refer to any word from Jesus, nor was the Old Testament the basis for its deliberations. The issue was decided on the basis of the Council's own authority! What *we believe* was determinative (Acts 15:11). Only after the question had been discussed and decided did James add that Scripture was in harmony with the decision (as we should expect).

I saw from this that we do not need to prove the existence of the bishop's position from scratch, by a study of the history of the Church. Scripture itself indicates the direction of the apostles' thoughts on this matter. People guided by the Holy Spirit, not books, were to take over the apostolic responsibilities of leadership (Jn 16:13). The bishop in his office embodies the authority of Christ here on earth in matters of faith and morals, just as the apostles did originally. The time of new general revelation ended with the apostles, however. What the bishop passes on now is the revelation made to those apostles. When we look at history, we are merely looking for corroborating evidence of what has become known as "apostolic succession". We see the signs of it already in the first recorded decision of the apostles after Jesus left them for heaven and then again in the first Church Council, the Council of Jerusalem.

Is there any historical evidence that the apostles' expectations were fulfilled in the early development of the Church structure? Yes! Bishops were leading the Church even before the end of the apostolic period. From about 92–101, Clement I of Rome was acknowledged as the (single) bishop of Rome (third in succession from Peter). It is clear from his *Epistle to the Corinthians* that belief in apostolic succession (the passing on of the apostles' authority) was already widely accepted in the Church. He wrote, "Our apostles . . . gave instructions, that when these [bishops] should fall asleep other approved men should succeed them in their ministry" (*First Epistle of Clement*, 44). Ignatius of Antioch wrote in A.D. 98 that in each city "there is one bishop, along with the presbytery and the deacons" (*Epistle of Ignatius to the Philadelphians*, 4). This was just before his martyrdom at the hands of the Romans.

These men were given substantial power by Christ to lead the Church, but to my mind three of these powers are the most important. The first is the right to consecrate the elements in the celebration of the Eucharist. No one except a duly authorized bishop (or his priests) can consecrate at the Eucharist. Nowhere does Scripture imply that just any Christian who is sincere enough has the right or ability to do this. Some sacraments, such as baptism, can be administered by any Christian, but not the Eucharist.

The second power is the ability to pass on their office. This is presupposed in what the apostles did in Acts 1. The fact that there was no discussion of the matter so soon after Jesus had been teaching them lends credence to the Catholic position. Christ himself must have provided for succession when he taught the apostles during the time between his Resurrection and his Ascension.

The third power given to these leaders of the Church is recorded in John 20:22-23: "With that he breathed on them and said, 'Receive the Holy Spirit. If you forgive anyone his sins, they are forgiven; if you do not forgive them, they are not forgiven.'" Only God can forgive sins. Jesus demonstrated that when he was here on earth. But here Jesus explicitly delegates this power to the group of men who will lead his Church.

Before he delegates, however, he imbues them with God the Holy Spirit. Nowhere else in Scripture does Jesus ever do anything like this. In all of Scripture, the only similar event is found in the creation of mankind. God breathes into Adam, which makes Adam a living soul. Jesus here is creating in the disciples a new creation—the leadership of his Church. They are specifically endowed with powers that up to this time have been reserved for God alone. These are the historical and scriptural beginnings of the sacrament of Penance (also called reconciliation or confession).

Obviously, before the priest can forgive sins, he must hear them. That is presupposed in the power to forgive that Jesus bestows. As an Evangelical, I totally misunderstood the confessional and what it was all about. I now go to confession about twice a month. My confessor hears thousands of confessions each year. He wants no details or names. I may remain anonymous if I so desire. I know of no priest who enjoys hearing confessions. It is hard work. Priests do it to help people and to obey God.

No priest claims to forgive sins through his own power. He is standing in for Christ, as it were. Because Catholics believe deeply in the mystical body of Christ (Jesus referred to it and Paul explicitly taught it), they can say that in forgiving us Jesus uses one part of his body—the vocal chords of a particular priest. Based on the authority given to the Church's leaders, recorded in the above passage, it is the voice of Christ that we hear forgiving us during the sacrament of Penance. Because the Church's members—you and I as Christians— really, actually are Christ's mystical body here on earth, when we act for Christ in his service as he instructed, it is really Christ acting. So it really is Christ, in his mystical body, who forgives in the confessional.

Once I understood that the sacrament of Penance is rooted and grounded in the doctrine of the mystical body of Christ, I fell in love with it. The command of James now made so much sense: "Confess your sins to each other" (5:16). There is a basic human desire to hear the words of forgiveness in our ears when we have wronged someone we love. Colleen and I have always said the words "I forgive you" after a spat. Sin is essentially a rebellion against God, whom every Christian loves. In the sacrament of Penance, I am brutally honest with God about my sins, and I hear the forgiveness of Christ in my ear.

Confession to a priest strengthens me, clears my conscience, and helps me love God anew. This is not to say I always find it easy or enjoyable. For those who are sceptical, I can only borrow a phrase from my adolescence, "If you haven't tried it, don't knock it."

Perhaps I should mention that Evangelicals think it a scandal that the Catholic Church allows people who may be less than perfect to remain in the Church. Ever since the persecutions endured by the early Church, Christians have argued about how generously forgiveness should be offered to sinners. Yet Jesus taught his disciples that false believers would always be an integral part of his true Church. In the parables of the wheat and the tares and of the net and the fishes, Jesus specifically tells the leaders of his Church to expect counterfeit Christians. It is important to note how we are to handle these "weeds" in the Church. Jesus commands us to leave them in the Church and to let him separate them in the end. It is not the Church's responsibility to tear out every weed or to throw back every bad fish (Mt 13:24–30, 47–52). This is a hard teaching for Evangelicals because of their penchant for corporate purity. Evangelicals have developed a reputation for "shooting their wounded". The Catholic Church takes a lot of heat for her willingness to proffer forgiveness, but she is being faithful on this issue to the teaching of our Savior.

The priest does not have authority to forgive sins independently of his bishop. As the Church grew, it became impossible for the bishop to celebrate the Eucharist and to hear confessions for everyone personally. Priests are ordained as assistants to the bishop. They have only those responsibilities delegated to them by the bishop.

I have encountered good assistants of the bishop and others who were not so good. I was utterly devastated by the advice given me by the first priest I asked for counsel. He informed me that he would never tell someone that it is wrong to abort a fetus, to masturbate, or to use birth control. He went on to inform me that he saw no good reason for me to do what I was planning. He felt the risks far outweighed the benefits of reconciliation to the Catholic Church. I wondered, "Am I the only person who believes Catholic teaching? And I'm not even Catholic yet!"

Even now the thought of this priest's words wounds me. I know I can never condone his counsel, yet at the same time it is not my responsibility to judge him. Many Christians experience a crisis of faith sometime during their pilgrimage, but God remains faithful. If we continue to strive to follow Christ, he helps us all, clergy and laity alike, grow into a fuller image of what we should be.

This experience helped me see where apostolic authority actually rests. It resides in the bishop and his office. A particular priest has no authority to teach what is not in agreement with the bishops' teaching. Since most of what a priest says during Mass is written in the missal, it is not difficult to ascertain when a particular priest is toying with heterodoxy. Simply be aware of any words he changes as he prays and speaks from the missal. Whenever he changes something, he is overstepping his authority. He is outside the teaching of the Church. But the experience of Jesus with Judas shows us that even a traitorous priest or bishop cannot destroy God's Church. God can always bring good out of evil.

Just after I had informed my Evangelical pastor of what I was contemplating, the archbishop of our archdiocese was sued by a man alleging sexual abuse. For my personal pilgrimage, the news came at an inopportune time. I remember taking an hour at lunch and going to a church to pray. While there, I realized that the archbishop's guilt or innocence was irrelevant to my decision. I was not following any particular person or even the teachings of a single person. God was calling me to join his Church, with all the imperfect people who may be a part of that Church. Catholics admit their sinfulness every time they participate in Mass. Our archbishop was later exonerated when the man apologized and admitted that his memories were completely untrustworthy (possibly implanted by hypnosis).

What I am saying is that the office of bishop is the basic building block of Church hierarchy. Priests must stay in communion with their bishops' teachings, and bishops need to stay in communion with the teaching of the pope and their fellow bishops. Of course, the pope has Scripture, tradition, prior popes, and the councils to guide him. In all of them, God the Holy Spirit is essential in his role as protector of truth. None of these present players is perfect, nor do they make any claim to be. That is good, because neither am I.

I should add that the vast majority of priests I encounter are wonderfully faithful to the teaching of the Church. I have never personally met a "Judas priest". Priests give up a great deal for their vocation; they love God and the Church deeply. As an Evangelical, I had no idea how much time every priest is required to spend in prayer each and every day.

Catholics call their priests "Father" out of respect for their leadership. We are, after all, the family of God. This family, like most other families, is a benevolent dictatorship. Many decisions that the priest makes alone would be, in Evangelical churches, agonized over by a group. While some may criticize this system, I find it refreshing. It frees the Church to do the important work of ministry.

I used to think that Matthew 23:9 prohibited this Catholic practice: "Do not call anyone on earth 'father'." On further thought, I remembered that Evangelicals call people "Sunday School teacher" and "Bible teacher" in spite of the very next verse: "Nor are you to be called 'teacher', for you have one teacher, the Christ" (Mt 23:10). Even Paul wanted to be thought of as the father of his spiritual children: "My dear children . . . I became your father through the gospel" (1 Cor 4:14–15). Jesus is obviously not prohibiting the use of "father" as Catholics use it. We are family.

V

Authority Focused

Once we understand that the bishop's office (or See) is a means of passing down the authority, responsibilities, and privileges of the original apostles, the next logical question is "Does Scripture give us any hint that perhaps one apostle, and the bishops succeeding to his office, was given more leadership responsibility for the Church's welfare?" The answer is an unqualified "Yes." In fact, this preeminence of one bishop's office was so clear from the beginning that it is the only bishopric still associated with that original apostle's name. I am referring to the "See of Peter", located in Rome. That this was Peter's See is substantiated in writings as early as the second century (Hegessipus' list).

There are several passages that show Peter being given this greater responsibility for the leadership of the Church. The scriptural evidence is so clear, in fact, that a professor I studied with at TEDS admits to Peter's primacy among the apostles (Dr. D. A. Carson in *God with Us* and in his contribution to *The Expositor's Bible Commentary* on Matthew).

One scriptural passage more than any other is pivotal:

"But what about you?" he asked. "Who do you say I am?" Simon Peter answered, "You are the Christ, the Son of the living God."

Jesus replied, "Blessed are you, Simon son of Jonah, for this was not revealed to you by man, but by my Father in heaven. And I tell you that you are Peter, and on this rock I will build my church, and the gates of Hades will not overcome it. I will give you the keys of the kingdom of heaven; whatever you bind on earth will be bound in heaven, and whatever you loose on earth will be loosed in heaven" (Mt 16:13–20).

Up until this time in the book of Matthew, Jesus had not claimed to be the Messiah or allowed others to make that claim in his presence. Jesus had not even told John the Baptist directly who he was when John specifically asked that question on the eve of his martyrdom. This passage is a climax to the first part of Matthew. Jesus finally acknowledges that he is the long-awaited Messiah.

"Blessed are you" is not a normal way of addressing someone. In Scripture, Jesus uses it to address a particular person only once—in this passage. He uses the expression elsewhere only in the generic sense, to encourage us to exhibit a certain trait (for example, "Blessed are the poor"). Jesus is clearly drawing attention to what he is about to say to Peter in front of the other disciples. Prefacing it this way gives it the aura of being the most important statement he ever makes to Peter (or to anyone else, for that matter). Any attempt to minimize the implications of the rest of this passage must first deal with how Jesus begins this address to Peter.

Mary is the only other person addressed in this manner in the New Testament. Elizabeth says "Blessed are you among women" under the inspiration of the Holy Spirit, when she greets Mary as "the mother of my Lord" (Lk 1:42, 45). Mary is addressed this way when Elizabeth publicly declares that Mary will be a mother—of the Christ. Peter is addressed this way when Jesus publicly declares that Peter will be a father—of the Church of Christ.

Peter did not conclude that Jesus was Messiah on the basis of his own experience or his superior intellect. This is important. God the Father intervened in history to reveal it directly to Peter: "This was not revealed to you by man, but by my Father in heaven." This revelation from God, and Peter's willingness to verbalize it, is what separates Peter from the other disciples from this point forward. Jesus' words in verses 18 and 19 are all addressed to the second person singular. There could be no mistaking that what Jesus said was meant for Peter alone. All the successors of the apostles would have supernatural powers and responsibilities, but Peter's would be special.

First of all, Jesus calls Peter by his new name. Jesus renamed Simon to emphasize the qualities of this new name. This would be analogous to my naming a friend "spaghetti-head" because his hair is always tangled and sticky. The only purpose for my doing it is to emphasize a trait. "Spaghetti-head" draws attention to a personal trait. A name can also emphasize a position or a role. That is what Jesus is emphasizing in this passage: Peter's new role.

"Peter" is a transliteration; the word Jesus used was "rock". Evangelicals point out that in the Greek text of this passage there are two words for rock: that referring to Peter is masculine, while that referring to the foundation of the Church is feminine. Because of these differences, Evangelicals teach that the foundation rock of the Church is the *faith* of Peter, as opposed to Peter himself. Peter's faith was the focus of this promise, not Peter. Even as an Evangelical, I thought this seemed an odd way for Jesus to express himself. Why make all these promises to Peter if "rock" refers to the faith, not the man? To claim the rock was Peter's faith seemed to me to make nonsense of the rest of the paragraph.

The insurmountable problem with the Evangelical analysis of the Greek text is that in Aramaic, the language of Jesus, there was only one word for rock (*Kepha*). The Greek text is itself a translation of the original Aramaic. There was no possibility of the original hearers being confused about Jesus' meaning. The disciples had to have heard Jesus saying, in Aramaic, "I tell you that you are Rock (*Kepha*), and on this Rock (*Kepha*) I will build my church." There is not the slightest room for any other meaning in the words Jesus originally uttered! The Church would be built on Peter as "rock", as distinguished from the other apostles there that day with him. The Aramaic word for "rock", transliterated into English, can be written *Cephas*. That this name for Peter is used elsewhere in Scripture lends further support for the Catholic understanding of this passage (see Jn 1:42; 1 Cor 1:12, 3:22, 4:5, 15:5; Gal 2:9–14).

So why would the translator (in this case Matthew) use two different words with two different genders? The reason seems rather simple. The best translation for the Aramaic "rock" was a feminine Greek word meaning "large rock". The problem with using that same word for a man's name is obvious. Naming Peter "Petrina" would be awkward. Faced with this problem, often inherent in translations, Matthew chose another Greek word for "rock", a masculine word. We are not used to these gender problems in English, but they are common in many languages. In English the Greek would be roughly equivalent to "I tell you that you are Rocky (masculine), and on this Rockette (feminine) I will build my Church."

For centuries no group seriously called into question whether the rock that was the foundation of the Church was the same as the rock that was Peter. Christians understood the

Aramaic background out of which the Greek was derived. Only recently, in attempting to understand this passage in isolation from its original roots, have Christians been confused.

Jesus now establishes four promises to Peter. First, Christ's Church will be built on Peter: "On this rock I will build my Church."

Second, all the power of hell will not defeat this Church: "The gates of Hades will not overcome it."

The third promise to Peter involves keys: "I will give you the keys of the kingdom of heaven."

Last, Peter is granted special authority: "Whatever you bind on earth will be bound in heaven, and whatever you loose on earth will be loosed in heaven."

These four promises are in the second person singular. Nowhere else does Jesus extend all four of these promises to the other disciples. They all understood that Peter was being singled out for special authority. Peter let it go to his head (as it might have to mine as well) in Matthew 16:22. This lapse, however, could not alter Jesus' promise that Peter's role, and that of his successors, was unique. As we will see, Jesus is establishing Peter's office, which is more important than any single person, including even Peter himself.

From the first promise we see that Jesus will be the person building the Church on Peter: "On this rock I will build my church." The implications of this hit me one day like a load of bricks. I know many talented Evangelicals who are building organizations "for the glory of God". They are very devout, very ambitious, and some of them are very successful. At one time, I was putting my shoulder to the plow alongside some of them. But are these people helping Christ build his Church on the rock that Christ chose? On Peter? I had to answer "No." Instead, many of my friends were taking sheep out of Peter's fold and into their own organizations. They have many justifications for being outside Peter's Church, but I have no stomach for tearing down the work Jesus promised he himself would build.

Integral to the word-picture behind this first promise is the implication that if the rock is tampered with, the Church will crumble, and that if the Church is moved, she will be without the foundation Christ himself chose. The Church Christ was building on Peter cannot be reduced to a mere set of ideas and beliefs. Does anyone ask which of the many churches today is Christ's true Church? Look for Peter or his direct successor.

To be in communion with the Church founded on Peter guaranteed that I was in the Church Christ himself was building. The second promise of Christ to Peter tells me that this will always be the case: "The gates of Hades will not overcome it." This promise reaches into the future, into the twenty-first century and beyond. What will not be overcome? The Church founded on Peter.

This promise cuts right to the heart of the Reformation. Could the Church Jesus founded ever become so corrupt that it would be better to abandon her? Would anyone ever be justified in taking the ideas of Jesus and separating themselves from this original institution because of her imperfections? Would the powers of hell ever weaken this Church founded on Peter to the point where the institution herself was a hopeless case? No. Jesus chose his leaders. New leaders are ordained in each generation. Jesus promised to preserve *that* Church from being subverted by hell's powers. I saw that nowhere does Scripture give justification for the split that occurred at the Reformation. This realization struck me with such force one day that it actually hurt physically.

The Church may be strong in some periods of history and weak at others. Many Catholics would agree that the Church in America has seen better days. Be assured, the Church universal has also seen much worse. What the second promise of Jesus tells me, however, is that I need not lose sleep over whether the Church founded on Peter will die or apostasize. All the power of hell itself will never obliterate Christ's Church.

There is no use in bemoaning the present situation. The useful response is to get in there and help! The Church needs more people like Joseph of Arimathea and Nicodemus. When prospects for the success of Jesus' Kingdom were at their worst, when there was no personal advantage to be gained for themselves or their families, in the spiritual blackness and confusion that enveloped the night we now call Good Friday, these two men publicly rallied to Jesus' side and buried him. O God, we need men like that in your Church today!

The promise of the keys is the only one of the four that is not relatively clear on first reading: "I will give you the keys of the kingdom of heaven." Twentieth-century Evangelicals tend to superimpose their own cultural milieu on this part of the passage. Because we all carry keys nowadays (I count seven in my own pocket), and the major purpose of those keys is to open doors, we assume that Jesus was giving Peter the right to open something for someone. One common misconception is that this promise was fulfilled when Peter opened the gates of the Church first to the Jews and then to the Samaritans and the Gentiles.

But if we accept this explanation, we ignore a very important rule for understanding the Bible. The best method of interpreting the Bible is by using the Bible. There are only two Old Testament uses of the word "key". One of these is in

Isaiah 22:22: "I will place on his shoulder the key to the house of David; what he opens no one can shut, and what he shuts no one can open." Compare that with Jesus' words in Matthew: "I will give you the keys of the kingdom of heaven; whatever you bind on earth will be bound in heaven, and whatever you loose on earth will be loosed in heaven." If you think the passages are similar, you are not alone. Even evangelical Old Testament commentaries admit that Jesus was borrowing the words of Isaiah to give meaning to his words to Peter.

What did Isaiah mean by these words? Isaiah was speaking to Eliakim, a new "prime minister" in Israel. Eliakim took over the office from an unworthy prime minister. God was telling Eliakim that he would be chief ruler in Israel, under the king alone. Isaiah uses two images in his discussion, a key and a peg. It is evident in Isaiah 22:22 that the key has two important aspects. It is a symbol of the power to rule—authority, and it symbolizes permanence—intergenerational succession. The key existed prior to being given to Eliakim, and it would exist after Eliakim passed on. The key, the power to rule, passes from mortal to mortal.

Later in Isaiah a peg is used to signify the instability of Eliakim's personal position. The peg, Isaiah foretells, will be pulled down: Eliakim would be cut down in the prime of his rule. The peg relates to Eliakim on a personal level. But the key denotes an *office*, both power-full and permanent.

It is significant that Jesus uses only the symbolism of the key with Peter and never the peg. Peter is to be chief ruler in the new Israel (as Paul calls the Church), under the king alone (Christ). The fact that Jesus gives Peter the keys of the Kingdom symbolizes Peter's power to rule, just as it did in Isaiah. This is the authority of Peter's office. His authority will be passed down, just as the authority of the other apostles will be passed down as they die. This is the intergenerational succession of Peter's See. The office of the key survives the death of any one man.

Jesus made Peter the earthly leader of his Church. Because Scripture calls the Church a family, we can call Peter and his successors the spiritual fathers of God's family on earth. Peter could be said to be the new, earthly high priest of the new Israel. With the giving of the keys, a new authority structure is instituted for the people of God. As in Isaiah, there occasionally may be unworthy persons in possession of these keys, but the position is greater and more permanent than any one person. The office will survive and continue.

G. K. Chesterton made an interesting point by observing that keys are unique and cannot be altered without making them useless. It is no good saying that the shape of a certain key doesn't please me, and so I will file it down. If I change the key, I make it useless for its original purpose. Some Evangelicals wish that Rome's authority within the Catholic Church were less complex, or less physical, or less spiritual, or less worldly, or less something else. They yearn for the elusive "simple religion of Jesus". We must never forget, however, that it is not our prerogative to demand change to suit our fancy. The keys to rule the Church permanently were given to Peter and to his successors in Rome, not even to the other apostles, let alone to me. If I refuse the key provided, I have only myself to blame if I fumble at the door.

Jesus' fourth promise to Peter fills in a few details about the power to rule the Church: "Whatever you bind on earth will be bound in heaven, and whatever you loose on earth will be loosed in heaven." This is a very broad promise. John Chrysostom, one of the four great Fathers of the East and leader of the Church in Constantinople in 398, wrote an early commentary on the New Testament. He wrote of this passage: "The Son granted to Peter over all the earth a power which is that of the Father and of the Son himself, and gave to a mere mortal man authority over all that is in heaven, in giving the keys to the same" (quoted in Thomas Aquinas, *Contra errores graecorum*). Peter and his successors are given explicit permission to bind and loose Christians in matters of faith and morals. Heaven and Peter will rule in concert. Because of the special protection given by the Holy Spirit to Peter, his decisions (within certain parameters) will always be in agreement with heaven.

It is difficult for many Evangelicals to give their obedience to another human. I remember Evangelical friends demanding the chapter and verse for everything. If we personally could not see the importance of an issue, we hesitated to give it our attention. I came to understand, however, that Peter's authority to bind and loose things in heaven was not at all contingent on my ability to comprehend his motivations or reasoning. I am not a crucial part of this equation. Jesus says that if Peter binds it, it is bound in heaven—period. I cannot think of a better way for Jesus to have said that Peter is to rule the Church. This power goes far beyond advice or honor. Binding and loosing denote power to compel, and the power to compel is the essence of the power to rule. (All those who hesitate at this should ponder the IRS.)

According to this fourth promise, Peter and those in his succession are not limited simply to enforcing an unchanging religion established in the first century. In Peter's power to rule it is clear that Jesus explicitly gives him the authority to change things. This promise was extended to the other apostles as a group in Matthew 18:18: "Whatever you bind on earth will be bound in heaven, and whatever you loose on earth will be loosed in heaven."

Some Christians have claimed that the changes since Vatican II have been so great that the Church will not survive. That there has been change is undeniable, but the changes are not so earth-shattering as some fear.

While doing beach evangelism in 1976, I met a Franciscan. His peace and holiness would have impressed anyone, but I still attempted to share the gospel with him. He gave me a Catholic introduction to theology that had been published in the 1930s. I did not read it until recently. I compared all the "changes" that were a result of Vatican II against this pre-Vatican II publication. I found that most of the changes being trumpeted about were not changes at all. They were already integral to the thought contained in the earlier publication.

Evangelicals have to remember that after every major council of the Church there has been a time of readjustment. Some historians claim it takes a hundred years or more for the Church to absorb the truths expressed in each new council. After the Council of Nicaea, for example, there were more Arians than there had been before the Council declared Arianism to be heretical. By defining the heresy, the Council strengthened the resolve of the heretics. Centuries later, we all agree that Arianism is heretical.

This is not to say, however, that change has not occurred as a result of Vatican II. Change has occurred and will continue to occur. This was an important issue to me, because I felt that no organization could be the true Church if it contradicted itself on essential doctrines over time. I spent quite a bit of time thinking this over. Here are my observations.

Since change is a very general term, let us separate it into two parts. There is a change that expands on prior truths without negating them, which I will call "development". This type of change "unpacks" the hidden meaning inherent in the original truth so that the truth can be understood better. It defines. The other type of change reverses that which has been accepted originally. I will call that type "contradiction". Contradiction affirms one day that "A" is true, and the next insists that "non-A" is true.

There is one other distinction we must make. In thinking through this issue for my own edification, I came to see that the information of the Church could be divided into at least five categories: deposit, dogma, doctrine, discipline, and devotion. I devised these categories for my own thinking, so I suppose the alliteration proves that I once studied homiletics. These are not the categories of the Church herself, but merely distinctions that helped me clarify the idea of change.

Deposit is that body of truth originally given to the apostles. In time, some of it was written into Scripture, while some of it remained in its original form of oral tradition. Protecting this deposit is a major responsibility of the bishops. The Church teaches that nothing can be added to or contradicted within the deposit. For example, Peter had no authority to make up a new story about Jesus healing someone. General revelation ended with the death of John, the last apostle. The goal regarding the deposit is simply to conserve it with no change whatsoever. As an Evangelical, I was surprised at how seriously Catholics regard this responsibility.

Dogma is that body of truth that has been affirmed by the councils of the Church and the Holy See of Rome. The further explanation, definition, and development of the concepts within the deposit, as well as the deposit itself, are contained within dogma. Once dogma is declared by the bishops, it can be further developed but never contradicted by future doctrine or dogma. I could find no case within Vatican II where earlier dogma was contradicted.

Dogma is usually declared in council or by the pope to combat a particular problem. For example, the dogma regarding the divinity of Christ was not declared by council until teachers in the early Church questioned that truth of the deposit. The deposit always contained the truth of Christ's divinity, however. The Council of Nicaea certainly did not invent new truth about Christ's nature as God-man. They merely clarified the truth already believed. So, dogma can be developed.

Doctrine is the development of truth on the basis of the deposit and dogma. Doctrine can develop and even contradict itself over time, because it is largely the thoughts of people. It has not been officially declared true or false by the Church. This is the realm in which most theologians deal, on the cutting edge of the Church's thinking. One Catholic theologian may totally contradict another equally Catholic theologian. They both can't be right, yet the Church is withholding her judgment on that particular issue. More thought, more wisdom, or more time may be needed before the Church decides which formulation of that particular doctrine is fully consistent with the deposit and dogma. Doctrine pushes the envelope of the Church's thought and is only slowly, if ever, accepted as dogma.

Otherwise good, careful Evangelical scholars make the mistake of taking doctrine as the unchangeable teaching of the Church. When they see it changing over time, they draw the wrong conclusions. The reason is relatively simple. The ultimate authority in most Evangelical churches of what is truly biblical rests with those men teaching at the seminary from which that church draws its pastors. If the pastor and board get into a theological tussle over some issue, it is not unusual for a seminary professor to be called in to moderate and to decide the truth in question. As a result, when these same Evangelical scholars attempt to understand what is really going on inside the Catholic Church, they make the mistake of looking to their counterparts in the Catholic seminaries as the authorities on Catholic theology.

It seems that every Evangelical pastor has at least one anti-Catholic book in his study. When I informed my pastor of my intentions, he lent me a book written by a professor at TEDS who is now at another institution. This truly fine scholar stumbled rather dramatically in his research because he made precisely the mistake of considering professors as the authorities. In the Catholic Church the professor is not the final arbiter of truth; the bishops and the pope are. The Church's pronouncements are very accessible, but most Evangelicals don't ever read these documents, much less footnote them, in their discussions of what Catholics teach. You do not know what Catholics teach unless you go to the sources that they themselves accept as authoritative.

Disciplines are those rules that govern the everyday life of faithful Catholics. This area has seen the most change (contradiction) in our generation, and it is this very visible area that people usually point to when they accuse the Church of having changed since Vatican II. For example, in the past, Catholics were required to fast on the Ember Days, twelve days each year. They are no longer required to do this.

This is a bitter pill for Evangelicals to swallow, but disciplines are supposed to be mandatory when in force, yet some of them may be changed over time. It would have been wrong for a Catholic to ignore the Ember Days fast in the 1950s. Yet now it is no longer necessary to fast on the former Ember Days (except Good Friday) because this discipline has been rescinded. Why? It has to do with obedience.

As Christians, we are under the authority of the apostles' successors, the bishops. They are responsible for making rules that will enhance the spiritual life of their flock. Although that goal never changes, the rules of discipline may. When the bishops decide an existing rule is no longer effective in helping people worship God, or when they determine that a new rule would be effective, it is a Catholic's duty to obey them. This is certainly in line with the promise: "Whatever you bind on earth will be bound in heaven, and whatever you loose on earth will be loosed in heaven." Disciplines by their very nature are going to be developed and contradicted over time—bound when the need arises and loosed when appropriate.

Devotions are the most personal of these five categories. Devotions are those activities by which an individual Christian may enhance his walk with God. The Catholic use of "devotion" is much broader than the Evangelical use of the word. It means much more than Bible study and prayer. Devotions are never mandatory for a Catholic layman, although they may be approved and are highly recommended. History illustrates that devotions develop over time.

One well-known example of a devotion is the Rosary. I remember being relieved to learn that a practicing Catholic could choose never to say the Rosary and still be a good Catholic. A priest friend helped me understand that Christ and his sacrificial death are at the very center of Catholic worship. The Rosary is only about eight centuries old. Most Catholics, however, wonder why anyone would choose not to speak with Mary. As a devotion, the Rosary is approved by the Church, but it is never mandated. Devotions can develop.

After researching this issue of change, I came to the conclusion that the Catholic Church is correct in her assertion that the pope is the touchstone for orthodoxy today. The changes of recent years are all within the scope of what Jesus intended in his promises to Peter. Nothing within the original deposit of faith can ever be contradicted, but the gospel

must be proclaimed to each successive generation in ways
that draw us to God.

While wrestling with this issue of change, I encountered
other Scripture passages that tell us more about Peter and his
See.

Just before the Passion, Jesus said to Peter, "Simon, Simon,
Satan has asked to sift you as wheat. But I have prayed for
you, Simon, that your faith may not fail. And when you have
turned back, strengthen [confirm] your brothers" (Lk 22:32).

The fact that Satan has a particular interest in Peter is not
surprising when we consider the authority given Peter. If
Peter could be forced into heresy, Jesus' promise that the gates
of hell would not overcome his Church would be forfeit. It is
interesting that Jesus commands Peter to confirm his fellow
apostles after the events of the Passion are over. If there were
any doubts about the ruling primacy of Peter, the power of
Peter to confirm the other leaders of the Church should lay
them to rest.

After his Resurrection, Jesus singled out Peter, restored
him, and commanded him to "Feed my sheep" (Jn 21:15–
17). Here Peter is given the ultimate responsibility for the
spiritual teaching of the flock of God, Christian men and
women.

If we compile what we have discussed in Scripture itself
about the pope, the bishop of Rome in the See of Peter, this
is what we have so far. Out of all the apostles, the Church
will be built on Peter as foundation. He will rule the Church
via his power to compel, bind, loose, change, teach, and
confirm the other leaders of the Church. Because of Peter's
position, Satan is particularly interested in destroying him and
his Church, but Christ himself will not allow that to happen.

As with other issues regarding the leadership of the
Church, we should not feel we need to prove the primacy of

Peter and his successors from scratch when we look to history. From a historical perspective, Jesus and his statements are earlier than any other source. All Evangelicals would agree that the Gospels also have the advantage of being absolutely trustworthy. We have briefly looked at what they say. Is there confirmation when we look to Church history after Scripture's time?

Absolutely. Perhaps the earliest is in the *Epistle to the Corinthians,* written by Clement I, bishop of Rome about A.D. 97. It is important to remember that Clement wrote to a distant Eastern church, in Corinth, which had been founded by the Apostle Paul. The church in Corinth was also not far from where the last living apostle, John, resided. But when we look at what Clement wrote, there is no hint of his feeling that he was overstepping his authority. Nor is there any record that the Corinthians felt that way (nor, for that matter, has anyone since). Clement dealt with their internal Church affairs even more than with theology. If the ruling power of the keys had not already been recognized, this would have been outrageous. It was not considered outrageous precisely because it was believed to be the right of Peter's successor, from the beginning, to instruct and guide the entire Church.

Clement I chastised a church outside his geographical jurisdiction with his letter. The fact that the church accepted the chastisement tells us more than any formal justification ever could. This is not merely an argument from silence but an argument from what Clement actually did.

One other issue concerning the pope needs to be clarified for most Evangelicals. It relates to the claim of papal infallibility. Catholics do not believe that the pope is perfect, or faultless, or sinless, or even necessarily good, holy, wise, or nice. There have certainly been popes who have made foolish mistakes, enacted ruinous policies, or been bona fide scoundrels. There is one thing, however, that no pope has ever done in all history, from Peter to the present day. No pope has ever taught heresy.

Catholic belief in the infallibility of the pope is much the same as Evangelical belief in the infallibility of Scripture. When the pope, as head of the Church, proclaims doctrine, he will not be mistaken in his teaching. This does not mean he cannot make mistakes concerning other topics. This does not mean his teaching will be as good as it could be. This does not mean he will always have the wisdom or the courage to teach the truth when he should. What it does mean is that the teaching that is done will never be in error (heretical).

As an Evangelical, I always accepted the infallibility of Paul or Peter or John when they wrote their epistles. This did not mean, however, that they were faultless in their daily lives or in their conversations. Infallibility applied only to their ca-nonical writings. No one ever claimed that the apostles were perfect. It is much the same with the infallibility of the pope. The pope is infallible only when teaching under very specific, intentional conditions. Infallibility, as it applies to the popes, however, is a much rarer phenomenon than it is for the writers of Scripture. Only twice in the last two centuries has a pope infallibly declared Church teaching in an exercise of this extraordinary Magisterium of the Church (i.e., the pope speaking *ex cathedra*).

This belief of the Catholic Church is not taught explicitly anywhere in Scripture, but it is historically rooted in the Matthew passage already discussed:

"But what about you?" he asked. "Who do you say I am?" Simon Peter answered, "You are the Christ, the Son of the living God." Jesus replied, "Blessed are you, Simon son of Jonah, for this was not revealed to you by man, but by my Father in heaven. And I tell you

that you are Peter, and on this rock I will build my church, and the gates of Hades will not overcome it. I will give you the keys of the kingdom of heaven; whatever you bind on earth will be bound in heaven, and whatever you loose on earth will be loosed in heaven" (Mt 16:13-20).

If Peter is able to bind things in heaven itself, be enlightened by God the Father himself, and lead the Church in such a way that she will never be overcome by evil, then infallibility is an extremely modest conclusion to these promises. If the highest office of the Church taught error as truth, then how could it be claimed that hell had not succeeded against Christ's Church? Infallibility is rooted in the promise of Jesus and the guidance of the Holy Spirit.

As an Evangelical, I had always thought that the claim of papal infallibility was a power grab on the part of the pope. It would give any pope the power to fashion things just to his liking. What I came to see, however, is that the truth could not be more opposite. Infallibility is an entirely conservative doctrine. It means that no present or future pope can change (contradict) any dogma that has been accepted by the Church throughout her history. The teaching regarding the infallibility of the popes in faith and morals really gives the most power to the first pope, where it belongs. Each succeeding pope has slightly less latitude than his immediate predecessor. In an era when people have come to desire change for its own sake, this teaching assures us that the original dogma of the Church will be protected through the ages.

When we look for confirmation of this doctrine in history, we find it. Rome emerges as the only bishopric of the ancient sees that never taught heresy. Below is a chronological list of the bishops of four ancient sees for just a few hundred years. I have included Constantinople as an ancient see even though some people might not. Notice the frequent leadership of heretics in the other sees. Only Rome has always remained faithful to the original deposit of faith given to the apostles.

The date refers to the year the bishop took office. I have omitted any pretenders. Names of bishops in heresy I have put in italics; and the heresy is denoted as follows: AR = Arianism, MP = Monophysitism, MT = Monothelitism, and NE = Nestorianism. (Evangelicals would agree that these teachings are in fact heretical.) Those bishops in schism from the Roman Church I have indicated with the date in italics. The bulk of this list is taken from the best Church history I have ever read, the *History of Christendom* series by Warren H. Carroll (Christendom Press).

ROME	ANTIOCH	ALEXANDRIA	CONSTANTINOPLE
Silvester I 314	Eustathius 328	Athanasius 328	Alexander 317
	Paulinus 330 AR		
	Eulalius 330 AR		
	Euphronius 332 AR		
Mark 336	*Flaccillus 335* AR		
Julius I 337			Paul I 337
			Eusebius 339 AR
	Stephen I 343 AR		*Macedonius 342* AR
Liberius 352	*Leontius 344* AR		
	Eudoxius 358 AR		
	Ammonius 359 AR		
Damasus I 366	Meletius *361*		*Eudoxius 360* AR
	Paulinus 362		Evagrius 370
			Demophilus 370 AR
		Peter II 373	Gregory 379
Siricius 384	Flavian I 381	Timothy I 381	Nectarius 381
	Evagrius 388	Theophilus 385	
Anastasius I 399	Flavian I *393*		John IC 398

Innocent I 401	Porphyrius 404			*Arsacius 404*
	Alexander 413	Cyril 412		*Atticus 406*
Zosimus 417	Theodotus 417			
Boniface I 418				Sisinnius I 426
Celestine I 422	John I 428			*Nestorius* 428 NE
Sixtus III 432				Maximian 431
Leo I 440	Domnus 441	*Dioscorus I 444* MP		Proclus 434
	Maximus 449			Flavian 446
	Basil I 456	Proterius 452		Anatolius 449
	Acacius 458	Timothy III 460		Gennadios 458
Hilary 461	Martyrius 460			
Simplicius 468	Julian 471			Acacius 471
	John IIC 477			
	Stephen II 478			
Felix II 483	Calendion 481	John IT 482		Fravitas 489
Gelasius I 492	*Palladius 488* MP			*Euphemius 490*
Anastasius II 496	Flavian II 498	*John IIH 497* MP		*Macedonius II 496*
Symmachus 498	*Severus 512* MP	*John IIIN 505* MP		*Timothy I 511* MP
Hormisdas 514		*Dioscorus II 515* MP		
	Paul II 519	*Timothy IV 519* MP	John IIC 518	
John I 523	Euphrasius 521			Epiphanius 520
Felix III 526	Ephraem 526			
Boniface II 530				
John II 533				
Agapitus I 535				*Anthimius 535* MP
Silverius 536		*Theodosius I 536* MP		Mennas 536
Vigilius 538	Domnus III 545	Paul C 538		
		Zoilus 542		
Pelagius I 556	Anastasius I 559	Apollinaris 551		Eutychius 552
John III 561	Gregory 570	John IVP 570		John IIIS 565
Benedict I 575				Eutychius 578
Pelagius II 579		Eulogius 581		John IVF 582
Gregory I 590	Anastasius I 593			Cyriacus 595
Sabinian 604	Anastasius II 599			
Boniface III 607		Theodore S 607		Thomas I 607

Boniface IV 608	*Athanasius* 611 MP	John VA 609	*Sergius I* 610 MT
Adeodatus I 615			
Boniface V 619		George 620	
Honorius I 625	*John III* 631 MT	*Cyrus P* 631 MT	*Pyrrhus* 639 MT
Severinus 640			
John IV 640			*Paul II* 641 MT
Theodore I 642			
Martin I 649			
Eugenius I 655			

As is quite obvious from even this short list of bishops, the only sure way for the Christian to know that his doctrine was orthodox was to remain in agreement with the See of Rome. Take the years 512 to 518 as an example. Every bishopric succession except Rome had been overtaken by heresy. Why? Jesus made a promise to Peter, and he can be counted on to keep it.

There are many interesting historical illustrations of this protection to the Church provided by Christ through his Spirit. Once again, we must keep in mind that we are merely looking for confirmation, not proof. God has always protected the bishop of Rome from heresy, but sometimes it has been in spite of the actual man in office, and sometimes the margin of safety has been very slim. In many cases, the protection of God seems to be the only possible explanation. For my money, the most interesting story is that of Vigilius in the sixth century.

Theodora was the empress of the realm, ruling from Constantinople. She was a Monophysite, an adherent of a heresy that declared Jesus has only one nature, the divine. This heresy denies the human nature of Jesus, which Catholics and modern-day Evangelicals teach. Theodora determined to impose her thinking on the Pope, to bring him into line with the bishops of the East. Pope Agapitus, however, would not budge. While in Constantinople to remove a heretical Eastern bishop, he died. It seems likely that he was poisoned.

Vigilius, who very much wanted to be pope himself, was an assistant to Pope Agapitus. He met in secret with the empress and struck a deal with her. He agreed to enforce her heretical views regarding theology if she would force the Church to accept him as pope. After he was installed as pope, he would restore the bishop who had just been deposed by Pope Agapitus, even though that bishop had been dismissed as a Monophysite heretic. (It is extremely interesting that neither empress, emperor, Church, nor bishop questioned the authority of a pope to dismiss an Eastern bishop, as Agapitus had just done. They might poison the man, but they still did not dare to question the authority of the papal office.)

Before Vigilius could get back to Rome, however, Silverius was elected and installed pope after Agapitus. Silverius stood just as firm for orthodoxy as had Agapitus. He was subsequently accused (falsely) of treason and unlawfully stripped of his office by a secular general of Theodora's. Vigilius was present at the confrontation. Silverius would not resign, so he was banished to exile.

Vigilius took Silverius' place as though he were pope, although he could not be pope until the office was vacant. Vigilius was, in fact, an antipope. In spite of this, he promptly started to fulfill his promise, writing letters promoting the heresy of Monophysitism. The obvious problem he had, however, was that he could not be pope until Silverius was dead or had resigned. Vigilius seems to have made certain Pope Silverius did die, of starvation, about fifteen months after he had helped to exile him.

Reluctantly, the Church of Rome installed Vigilius as pope. To do anything else would have meant death or exile to

those involved. Theodora waited for her new pope to rein-
state her heretical bishop and to preach her heresy. He had
done just such preaching as antipope only a few short months
before. Now that he was recognized as pope, her plans could
come to fruition.

But God the Holy Spirit was working a most amazing
change in Vigilius. Whereas, as antipope, he had been enthu-
siastically defending Monophysite heresy, he now wrote the
empress a letter stating that he could never teach Monophysitism or support those who did, now that he was pope.
Vigilius then refused to approve a compromise solution ad-
vanced by the emperor himself. He must have known what
this could mean to him. Vigilius had participated in the murder of at least one pope over just this type of refusal to compromise with heresy. His moral character had been anything
but exemplary up to this point. He was guilty of both simony
and murder, yet God forgave him and provided him the grace
to endure his own martyrdom. While saying Mass in Rome,
Vigilius was arrested by the emperor's men and deported to
Constantinople. He never saw Rome again before his death,
ten exceedingly difficult years later. At no point after becoming pope, however, did Vigilius teach the heresy embraced by
the empress and most of the Eastern Church. Jesus had kept
his promise. The gates of hell skulked away empty handed—
the trophy had eluded it again.

In retrospect, I see that once I was convinced of the pope's
authority over Christian theology and the Church, it was
easier for me to accept this authority than it has been for
some other Evangelicals. I am not sure why. I have heard
Evangelical leaders state, "I would never accept another
man's spiritual authority over me!" or "Why should I follow a
man who wants to intrude even into my bedroom?" These
issues were never the crux for me. Did Christ set up a human

head for his Church here on earth? That is the question. When I was convinced, I submitted. What else was there to do? If Christ's representative here on earth made demands of me, I at least wanted to know what they were so I could attempt obedience.

Before that happened, however, I still needed to find out if this Church and the Bible were at odds in their dogma. I had always been under the impression that they were, yet I had to admit I had not done much primary-source reading of Catholic dogma. Most of my information about Catholic dogma had come to me filtered through other Evangelicals.

I took as a given, and I still do, that the Bible is never wrong in its teachings. That left three possibilities. Was the Church wrong in some dogma? Had I misunderstood the Church's teaching on some points? Was my understanding of the Bible wrong? I don't like to admit a mistake any more than the next guy, but it was not long before I realized that the last two questions were regularly being answered in the affirmative.

VI

The Bible

Most Evangelicals seem to have the impression that the Catholic Church does not appreciate the Bible. I remember one pastor friend laughing at the idea of Catholics attending a Bible study. Evangelicals are convinced that the Church sees the Bible as a competing authority and for that reason thinks access to the Bible should be restricted or at least discouraged. I shared this view of Catholicism for most of my adult life.

One of the aspects of Catholic worship that surprised me initially was the central role of the Bible in the worship service. Every Catholic church is on a three-year cycle of Scripture reading. A Catholic who attends Mass faithfully will hear almost all of God's word over a period of three years (with the exception of some genealogies, etc). That is a schedule most Evangelical churches would do well to emulate.

I tried to come up with some objective method of measuring the feelings of different churches for the Bible and what it says. I decided to time the percentage of Sunday morning worship spent in Scripture reading in three different types of churches. It seems plausible that the amount of time spent in the Bible would indicate regard for what it said. If a church spent no time in Scripture at all, it would be hard-pressed to demonstrate that it cared about what the Bible taught. I timed the services when the regular pastor was present, avoiding any special holidays that might distort the results. I did not count the time spent in talking about the Bible, just the time spent actually reading, singing, or reciting the inspired word itself.

I think Evangelicals will find the results surprising. I chose two large churches, one Evangelical and one fundamentalist, both with an average Sunday attendance reaching well into the thousands. The Evangelical church, in the northwest suburbs of Chicago, spent less than 6 percent of its Sunday service in Scripture. The fundamentalist church, in northwest Indiana, which considers itself to be biblically based, spent 2 percent of its morning in Scripture.

My own Catholic church would be very similar to any Catholic church in this country, because the missal is standardized. When I travel I can attend any parish church and know right where we are reading. Catholics at Mass spend more than 26 percent of the time in Scripture. Although exact percentages will vary from week to week, time in the Bible during Mass approximately quadruples the amount of time spent in the Bible during morning worship in the other two churches.

I am not implying that any of these churches should spend more time in Scripture. What is evident from this very small sample, however, is that Catholics hold the Scripture in very high regard. All would be better served if Evangelicals would freely acknowledge this fact. I do not think any church spends more time in Scripture than does the local Catholic parish.

Of course, individual Catholic devotion to Scripture is varied, as it is in the Evangelical community. I know Catholic laymen who spend from fifteen to sixty minutes every day in

Bible reading and prayer. Most of them, however, are much more reticent in discussing their relationship with God than are Evangelicals. Catholics seem to regard it as an encounter best kept private. Only after they have developed a good friendship with someone will they open up about their relationship with God. Granted, there are Catholics who never read the Bible. How are they any different from the many Evangelicals who have the same problem?

I have come to think that much of the misunderstanding between Catholics and Evangelicals about the importance of Bible reading, as with many other issues, arises from the fact that they use the same words to mean different things. This was a problem for me before becoming Catholic, so early on I bought myself a copy of Our Sunday Visitor's *Catholic Encyclopedia*. In my reading, I would look up the definitions of any words about which I had a question. Many times that definition would use additional words that I questioned. I found myself thumbing from definition to definition until I finally understood what was meant. I had to learn an almost entirely new vocabulary.

When an Evangelical discusses his personal Bible reading, meditation, and prayer time, he uses the word "devotions". This word means something totally different and much broader to a Catholic. If asked about his devotions, a Catholic is likely to start discussing the Rosary or the Forty Hours. The Evangelical is left with the misunderstanding that a Catholic never reads the Bible or prays to its ultimate Author.

When a Catholic discusses Bible reading and meditation, he uses the word "prayer" rather than "devotions". The new *Catechism of the Catholic Church* (CCC) is the definitive guide to Catholic teaching. It discusses three forms of prayer. Vocal prayer is that prayer composed of words, either spontaneous or memorized. The *Catechism* quotes John Chrysostom as teaching "Whether or not our prayer is heard depends not on the number of words, but on the fervor of our souls" (CCC 2700).

Second, meditation is the prayer of the Christian seeking "to understand the why and the how of the Christian life, in order to adhere and respond to what the Lord is asking" (CCC 2705). This type of prayer "tries above all to meditate on the mysteries of Christ, as in *lectio divina*", or sacred reading ("devotions" to the Evangelical). I have found that this is how most Catholics talk of Scripture reading, as a part of prayer.

Contemplative prayer is the third type of prayer discussed. It is "the simple expression of the mystery of prayer . . . a gaze of faith fixed on Jesus, an attentiveness to the Word of God, a silent love" (CCC 2724).

If Catholics do esteem the Bible highly, where did Evangelicals acquire this misperception that they do not? Where did Evangelicals get this firmly seated notion that the Catholic Church distrusts the Bible? Perhaps certain historical events have played a part. The Catholic Church as a whole has never forbidden reading the Bible, but a small group of bishops in medieval France did. They were trying to curtail heretics (called Cathars or Albigensians) who used the Bible to deny the Incarnation and humanity of Jesus and to teach Manichean dualism. They taught that marriage and child-bearing were wrong and that promiscuity, homosexuality, abortion, and even bestiality were good. Suicide was the preferred method of death. The medieval French bishops forbade the independent reading of Scripture as one way of attacking its misuse by these politically powerful heretics. When the heresy was eliminated, the prohibition was lifted. With the benefit of hindsight, we might argue that the bishops did not use the wisest methods for stamping out this destructive movement, but they did the best they knew how. Remember, no one ever claimed the leaders of the Church would be perfect.

One other historical incident that bothers Evangelicals is that the Catholic Church confiscated Bibles and burned them. Yes, the Church did do this. What seems to be forgotten, however, is the fact that they made replacement Bibles available. Evangelicals forget that the Bibles burned were poor translations. Even the most protestant of churches never refers today to the Tyndale Bible or the Wycliffe Bible. They were poor translations, and the Church was demonstrating her high regard for truth in rooting them out. Perhaps our techniques would be different in twentieth-century America, but one cannot fault the Church of that period. Her motive was to keep the truth pure.

The first Bibles were all produced by Catholics. The first person to translate any part of the Bible into English was the Catholic priest Bede, in the eighth century. Centuries later, the printer Gutenberg was a Catholic, and he printed the first Catholic Bible. In 1478, a Low German Bible was printed, so that any literate German could read it. By the end of the Middle Ages, much of the Bible was available in many European languages. Years later, even Luther admitted that without the Catholic Church we would not even have the Bible.

Of course, I always knew that these Catholic Bibles had extra books in them. Like most Evangelicals, I was totally misinformed about the historical background of what we called the Apocrypha. (Catholics refer to these books as deuterocanonical.) As I explored this issue, I was surprised by what I discovered. Finally, I began again at ground zero by separating out the facts that were not in dispute.

The Apocrypha question touches on the Old Testament

only. It relates to seven books (or portions) of the Bible included in the Catholic Old Testament but not in the Protestant version. New Testament books are not affected. (The New Testament has a separate canonical issue involving the Gnostic books. Evangelicals, unlike a small group of liberal Protestants, are in total agreement with Catholics on the New Testament canon.)

The Septuagint translation (of the Old Testament) was the accepted Greek Bible of the Jews in Palestine and elsewhere for well over a hundred years before Jesus' birth. Both Jews and Christians accepted it as their Bible for over half a century after the Ascension as well. Its canon (list of included books) is not in doubt. The Septuagint included the seven books of the Apocrypha on equal standing with the rest of the inspired Old Testament. There is no doubt that Jesus and his contemporaries all used the Septuagint.

The New Testament writers allude to these apocryphal books over two dozen times. Their use of these books as a source is indistinguishable from their use of much of the Old Testament (see Bruce Metzger, *An Introduction to the Apocrypha*). Some of the parallels are much clearer in Greek than in English. But even in English, James 1:19, "Be quick to listen, slow to speak", sounds very much like Sirach 5:11, "Be swift in listening, but slow in answering." The similarities between Paul's epistles and Wisdom are so striking that Ronald Knox even suggested that Paul might have written Wisdom.

This use of what Protestants call apocryphal (and Catholics term deuterocanonical) books by New Testament writers is not a departure from Old Testament precedent. The Old Testament refers to biblical and apocryphal characters with equal respect. For example, Ezekiel 14:14 and 20 refer to Noah, Job, and Daniel. As an Evangelical, I had always assumed that Ezekiel was referring to the Noah of Genesis 5–9, the Job of

Job 1–42, and the Daniel of Daniel 1–12. While I was correct about Noah and Job, the reference could not possibly have been to the Daniel I had thought. The Daniel of Daniel 1–12 was only a child when Ezekiel wrote. Ezekiel must have been referring to another Daniel, who was so well known to his audience that he needed no more explanation than did Noah or Job. We find this historical character in the Apocrypha, Daniel 13–14. This Daniel (sometimes spelled Danel) lived long before Ezekiel's time, and he was a Gentile, as were Noah and Job (CCC 58). Inspired by the Holy Spirit, Ezekiel wrote using the apocryphal books he had access to in the same manner as he used the rest of Scripture.

The early Church Fathers followed the apostles' lead in this matter, peppering their writings with references from the apocryphal books, generally using the Septuagint translation. The Septuagint, with its inclusion of the apocryphal books, was undeniably the Bible of the early Church.

There are Christian lists of the canon of Scripture, including the Apocrypha, from very early times. The first fragment of any canonical list appears to date from just after the end of the first century. The major early disputes, however, involved the canon of the New Testament. The canon of the Old Testament was not in dispute within the early Church.

Beginning with Peter's sermon at Pentecost, the Christians and the unbelieving Jews locked in battle over whether Jesus was the Jewish Messiah. The Christians made extensive use of Old Testament messianic prophecies. Many of these prophecies were in the seven books that Evangelicals now refer to as apocryphal.

The Jewish leaders revised their canon about A.D. 90 to exclude those books not written in Hebrew (2 Maccabees, Wisdom, and Daniel 13–14) and those books for which the Hebrew original was not extant (Judith, Baruch, Sirach, and

1 Maccabees), perhaps in order to solve much of their apologetical problem with the Christians. By excluding those books, they eliminated many messianic prophecies. This revision came to be called the Palestine Canon, but it was a *Jewish* canon, developed after many of the apostles were dead and most of the New Testament had already been written. The Christians did not confirm this decision, taken independently by the Jews.

In fact, Christians continued to use these seven books as before. Some early scholars questioned their validity, but they were prompted by Jewish objections to the validity of apocryphal messianic prophecies. Later Christians questioned some of these books, but they questioned some New Testament books as well. The Church as a whole continued using them because they had been accepted since the first century.

Those are the facts that all sides can agree on. What do they mean? When I started to think this issue through, I found myself becoming angry with my Evangelical teachers for the very first time! The conclusions followed so easily. It seemed to me that only someone who willfully ignored the obvious could come to Evangelical conclusions about the Apocrypha. Then I remembered that I too had ignored these facts for most of my life. I cooled down rather quickly.

It is a fact that Jesus, his apostles, the New Testament writers, and the early Church all used a Bible that included the Apocrypha. The Palestine Canon, which excluded these books, had not been "invented" yet. I recognized with a mental "thud" that the Catholic Church had not added these seven books after the Reformation in order to bolster their theology. On the contrary, councils of the Church had included the Apocrypha in the list of the canon long before the Reformation. The reformers took these books out of the canon accepted by the early Church. They accomplished this by borrowing a canon developed by non-Christian Jews more than a generation after Jesus' death and Resurrection.

Why would anyone do this? It seems that the reformers did not care for the teachings found in these books any more than did the non-Christian Jews of A.D. 90. The Jews had found the messianic prophecies objectionable. The reformers disliked the passages regarding salvation, prayers for the dead, and purgatory. They used the Palestine Canon as a precedent to delete these seven books, in spite of the fact that the Palestine Canon was not Christian. In addition, some reformers planned on printing editions of the New Testament without four books of the New Testament—Hebrews, James, Jude, and Revelation were to be relegated to an appendix. But without any precedent to point to, those four books were reinserted into the main body of the reformers' Bible. The seven apocryphal books, however, were never returned to the Old Testament.

Not all non-Catholic Bibles followed suit. The King James Version of the Bible originally included the apocryphal books. The Orthodox Churches accept these books. Even John Wesley quoted from them frequently in his revival sermons.

This raises a related issue. For Evangelicals and reformers alike, there are no objective criteria sufficient for faith. This is most obvious when we discuss the canon. Evangelicals have no good, objective explanation for accepting the canon they do accept. Catholics did not change the canon of the early Church or the deposit of faith to make them fit preconceived ideas. The fact that the reformers did is one of the saddest chapters in all Christendom.

When I realized this, for the first time in my life I was not sure how much I trusted Evangelical scholarship. From the timing of the different canons, it is obvious that Jesus used the

Septuagint, with its inclusion of those seven books. The early Church followed suit. Because, during the Reformation, the canon was being challenged, the Church reaffirmed the historic canon of the early Church in the Council of Trent. But to exclude books because they did not fit theological presuppositions struck me as outrageous. I loved the Bible too much for that, although I now knew I had seven extra books to explore.

I can't help smiling when friends ask me if I still read the Bible, now that I am a Catholic. The Bible is what drew me to the Catholic Church. Yes, I do still read it—all of it. So do many of my Catholic friends, every day.

VII

Salvation

As an Evangelical, I was involved in beach evangelism, college campus evangelism, street-corner evangelism, child evangelism, retirement home evangelism, rescue mission evangelism, mall evangelism, and door-to-door evangelism. I explained the plan of salvation many ways, including the "Roman Road", the *Four Spiritual Laws*, the messianic prophecies of the Old Testament, and the "Wordless Book". A major responsibility while I was in full-time Christian service was to train college students how to share their faith more effectively. Although I never considered evangelism my gift, I could not begin to estimate the number of people to whom I have witnessed (shared the gospel). Imagine the consternation I experienced when I first imagined that maybe, just maybe, I had not been sharing the same gospel as the original apostles.

Catholics universally accept Evangelicals as being truly Christian. The Church accepts Evangelical baptism as valid and sees Evangelicals as putting their faith into action in daily life. To a Catholic, these are sure signs that we are Christian brothers. Although we sometimes speak of "conversion", an Evangelical cannot convert to Catholicism. Strictly speaking, Evangelicals reconcile themselves to the Catholic Church.

Evangelicals, however, generally do not believe that all

Catholics are really Christians—some may be, but certainly not all. Evangelicals may desire Catholic cooperation on political or moral issues, but they do not consider Catholics to be Christian brethren. (Most Catholics I have met are shocked to learn this.) Evangelicals are alarmed that Catholics believe works are involved in the process of our salvation. Evangelicals have other areas of concern as well: baptism, purgatory, indulgences, and the necessity of having a personal relationship with God.

When I first explained our decision to reconcile with the Church to family and friends (over half of whom were ministers), I detected an interesting presupposition at work in almost every instance. After they came to terms with the fact that we were really going to do this and that they could bring up no objection with which we had not already wrestled, they assumed that we would remain "Protestant-Catholics". We would attend a Catholic church but still accept the two major tenets of the Reformation, *sola scriptura* (only Scripture) and *sola fide* (faith alone). The first tenet is a fairly straightforward issue, with which we have already dealt. At no point has an Evangelical been able to give me any convincing reasons to justify his faith in the sufficiency of Scripture.

As concerns soteriology (the study of Christian salvation), I hope only to shed some light on the issue from the perspective of an Evangelical who was reconciled to Catholicism. An in-depth theological approach is best left to the theologians, who write scholarly works. My goal in studying this issue was not to prove Catholic doctrine right and the Evangelical view wrong. My major premise was that, if Catholic dogma on salvation could be shown to be consistent with all of Scripture, then it should be given the benefit of the doubt. But I did not think that it could pass muster.

I approached the question in this way because, against my wishes, I had already come to Catholic conclusions concerning the Eucharist and authority. On these two issues Catholics were the only Christians who were incontrovertibly biblical. These two issues convinced me to become Catholic. On the issue of salvation, I was only checking to see whether Catholic dogma could be reconciled to the biblical data. If so, Catholicism had earned my trust so far, and I would accept the Catholic interpretation as true. I have a good friend who came to Catholicism from Evangelicalism from the opposite direction. The first issue that he was convinced about was soteriology.

What I found initially is that there is a tremendous amount of confusion on both sides of the discussion about what Evangelicals and Catholics believe. Many Evangelicals will tell you that they believe Christians are saved by faith. A few Catholics will tell you that they believe Christians are saved by works. Both are not only dead wrong, but both give inaccurate portrayals of their own theologies! Informed Evangelicals do not teach that we are saved by faith, and Catholics do not teach that we are saved by works.

Evangelical and Catholic theologies both accept as the starting tenet of soteriology that we are saved by *grace*. God gives us his life as an act of generosity on his part. This is not a point of disagreement between Catholics and Evangelicals. It is one of our glorious agreements! The hymn "Amazing Grace" is a favorite in both churches (and my personal favorite). None of us would have a chance at salvation but for the grace of God. We need to remind ourselves that on this point we are in total agreement. We are saved by grace. Anyone who disagrees with this analysis is not looking at the facts.

The *Catechism of the Catholic Church* puts it this way: "Since the initiative belongs to God in the order of grace, no one can merit the initial grace of forgiveness and justification" (CCC 2010).

As with so many terms, grace as defined by Catholics is slightly different from grace as defined by Evangelicals. As far as I can see, however, the difference is not crucial. Evangelicals define grace by referring primarily to its origin in God: grace is "the free generosity of God through the self-giving of Christ" (*The Zondervan Pictorial Encyclopedia of the Bible*). Catholics agree with this part of the Evangelical definition but go on to define how the grace of God affects us when we are touched by it: grace is "any divine assistance given to persons in order to advance them toward their supernatural destiny of fellowship with God. . . . Grace transforms a person's nature" (Our Sunday Visitor's *Catholic Encyclopedia*). Catholics will go even farther, distinguishing between *sanctifying* grace (supernatural life) and *actual* grace (supernatural aid).

But if we agree that we are saved "by" grace, "through" what are we saved? How does that grace of God become an active part of my life? That is the point at which Evangelicals and Catholics part company. We both call that part of the salvation process by its biblical term, justification. Justification prepares a Christian to meet a holy God in eternity. To phrase the question another way: "By" what are we justified?

Evangelicals define justification as an act of God whereby he declares the Christian righteous. It happens at one moment in time and is made possible by the Christian's faith alone (*sola fide*, justification by faith alone).

Catholics teach that justification starts at a moment in time but continues throughout a Christian's life. Justification is made operative in one's life by both faith and works. Some Evangelicals seem to imply that Catholics do not see a place for faith in justification. This is an error. The problem that Catholics have with Protestant soteriology is not the claim that we are justified by faith but the claim that we are justified by faith *alone*. The "alone" sticks in the Catholic craw. Catholics see it as an unnatural bifurcation of a seamless whole.

Let's summarize the difference another way. Catholics agree with Evangelicals that justification is by faith but not that it is by faith *alone*—works continue the justification after faith has begun it. Catholics agree with Evangelicals that justification has a starting point at a moment in time but not that justification ends at that moment in time: it continues throughout life. Some Evangelicals have likened Catholic justification to Evangelical justification and sanctification rolled up into one. A Catholic would respond that justification is not complete without complete sanctification: "Justification entails the sanctification of [man's] whole being" (CCC 1995).

As I researched this issue for my own satisfaction, there emerged two questions that could be answered only by going to Scripture. First, does Scripture indicate anywhere that works are essential for justification? If it clearly does so in even one passage, it would make the Evangelical position untenable and would strongly suggest that justification is more than just a momentary event. After all, works do take time. Secondly, does Scripture anywhere state that "by faith *alone*" we are justified? One clear statement such as this would be impossible to reconcile with the Catholic position on justification.

First, Scripture does clearly and emphatically teach that works are involved in the "by" of justification. The most obvious passage is in James:

What good is it, my brothers, if a man claims to have faith but has no deeds? . . . Faith by itself, if it is not accompanied by action, is dead. . . . You foolish man, do you want evidence that faith without deeds is useless? . . . Was not our ancestor Abraham considered right-eous for what he did when he offered his son Isaac on the altar? You see that his faith and his works were working together. . . . You see that a person is justified *by what he does and not by faith alone* (*James 2:14–26*).

I studied this passage in school, but when I look back on it I am amazed. In a classroom, you notice and remember what your professor thinks is important. It was only as an adult, when I was doing a careful study of James on my own, that I noticed that the Greek word used by James is unmistakable. It is the identical technical term used by all of the New Testament for justification. James said that a man is "*justified* by what he does".

This passage alone should put an end to the contention that we are justified by faith alone. Is it any wonder that some of the reformers attempted to put James into an appendix to the Bible rather than in its historically accepted place? It is interesting to me how many Evangelicals handle this passage. They ignore it! Or they mention it without incorporating its truth into their theology. They view it as a problem passage needing extensive explanation. This may be a reflection of an either-or mentality: that we must be justified by faith alone or by works alone. But neither James nor the Catholic Church claims justification comes by works alone. Justification is accomplished by faith coupled with works.

Our Sunday Visitor's *Catholic Encyclopedia* puts it this way:

> Justification in the Catholic Tradition comes about by means of faith in Christ, and in a life of good works lived in response to God's invitation to believe. . . . Catholic Faith holds that faith without good works is not sufficient to merit justification, for good works show one's willingness to cooperate with the initiatives of

grace.... What is necessary for salvation is a faith that represents itself both externally through acts and internally through faith.

If that sounds extremely familiar, reread James!

Most important, this is also the gospel of Jesus. His ideal was that of a life of good works flowing outward from a vibrant inner faith. The parables of the wise and foolish builders (Mt 7:24–27), the two sons (Mt 21:28–32), the good Samaritan (Lk 10:25–37), the talents (Mt 25:14–30), the sheep and the goats (Mt 25:31–46), and others all teach a unity of faith and works for salvation. Father Mitchell Pacwa, S.J., has made the point that the entire Sermon on the Mount is a discourse on Jesus' view of justification (justification and righteousness have the same root in Greek): "Not everyone who says to me, 'Lord, Lord,' will enter the kingdom of heaven, but only he who *does the will of my Father* who is in heaven" (Mt 7:21). How much more explicit could Jesus have been?

In the Lord's Prayer (also called the Disciple's Prayer and the Our Father), Jesus teaches us to ask God to forgive us in the same measure that we have forgiven others. "Forgive us our debts [trespasses], as we also have forgiven our debtors [those who trespass against us]" (Mt 6:12). Catholics pray this prayer in every Mass. Most Catholics (and "mainline" evangelicals) would be amazed to hear this, but I have never been in an Evangelical church that regularly recited the Lord's Prayer. I have participated in the worship services of literally hundreds of Evangelical churches. The theology of the Lord's Prayer just does not fit Evangelical notions concerning salvation. For this reason, they feel it is better left unsaid. As a teenager, I could have quoted entire chapters from the Pauline epistles, but I would have stumbled over this prayer. What a tragedy!

It is quite clear in Jesus' teaching that justification, and thus salvation, is accomplished in a unity of these two: faith and works. The whole process is made possible solely by grace. This is just what Catholic theology asserts.

Actually, there are a number of Evangelicals who have recognized this unity of faith and works and have incorporated the concept into their theology because they see it as scriptural. In the process, they have developed a very Catholic view of salvation. They don't seem to understand that their soteriology is Catholic! Many of them labor under the false assumption that Catholics believe in justification by works as *opposed* to faith. If they would just read Catholic theology for themselves, that misunderstanding could be remedied. The writings of some of the councils of the Church are a great place to start.

The second question I investigated, if answered in the affirmative, would make Catholic soteriology impossible: Does Scripture anywhere state that "by faith alone" we are justified? The long and the short of it is—no. Those words are never, ever used in relation to justification anywhere, by any of the New Testament authors. Because some Evangelicals imply that Paul does make this claim, we will begin with a short look at Paul's epistles.

It is important to keep in mind that Paul uses the word "works" in a very different way from either James or the Catholic Church. Generally, when Paul uses the word, he is using it to refer to Jewish obligational "works of the law". A good example of this is the important passage in Romans 4. Paul juxtaposes faith and works, but the works are explicitly stated to be those of the Old Covenant law, such as circumcision (Rom 4:9–15). This is very clear in Romans 3:28 as well: "For we maintain that a man is justified by faith apart from observing *the law.* Is God the God of Jews only? . . . There is only one God, who will justify the *circumcised* by faith and the uncircumcised."

This is obviously not what James or Jesus means by "works". Both of them (and the Catholic Church) agree that works must be tied to faith for the faith to be effectual and that both the faith and the works are solely the result of God's grace. This is obviously not the same as "works of the law". We could call the works of James and Jesus, which are necessary for faith to be effective, "graceful works". The Catholic Church has "graceful works" in mind when she refers to the works of justification.

Paul expresses this same thought, but he usually avoids the use of "work" as a noun, probably due to his continual struggles with the "party of the circumcision". In Philippians 2:12, he exhorts his converts to "work out your salvation with fear and trembling". Why "work", why "fear", and why "trembling", if faith is all that is necessary? Romans 6:22 expresses the same concept another way: "Now that . . . you have become slaves to God, the benefit you reap leads to holiness, and the result is eternal life." One more example: "God will give to each person according to what he has done. To those who by persistence in doing good seek glory, honor and immortality, he will give eternal life. But to those who . . . follow evil, there will be wrath and anger (Rom 2:6–8).

Although it is impossible to look at all the pertinent verses, two verses that Evangelicals advance as refuting Catholicism should be examined: "For it is *by grace* you have been saved, through faith—and this not from yourselves, it is the gift of God—not *by works*, so that no one can boast. For we are God's workmanship, created in Christ Jesus to do good works" (Eph 2:8–10). When I resigned from the Evangelical church where we had been members, I received a stinging letter quoting these verses. Evangelicals try to use this passage to prove that we are not saved by works. All a Catholic can do is agree! One of our glorious agreements is that we are *not* saved by *works*, we are saved by *grace*. That is what Paul is stating here. He is not pitting works against *faith*. The passage never tries to focus on the inner workings of justification. He is pitting works against *grace* (notice the use of the preposition "by", twice)! This verse says that we are saved by grace; that even the faith we have is a gracious gift; and that the works we do are nothing to boast of because they too are a gracious gift—"God's workmanship" in us. It is all grace through and through, from beginning to end. Catholics and Evangelicals alike love this passage. Let's just make sure we all understand its message correctly.

It was only after being reconciled to Catholicism that I found that some of the reformers had tampered with verse 8 to make it say what they wanted: they added the word "alone", making the verse say "saved through faith *alone*". The word "alone" is not in the Greek, nor in the context, nor is the idea conveyed by this changed verse found anywhere else in the Bible. I was reminded of an Evangelical apologetics professor who once stated, "All the cults start by tampering with the words of Scripture to make it say what they want." The words made me shudder when I remembered it in relation to the reformers' tampering with this verse.

Another verse commonly used against Catholics is Titus 3:5: "He saved us, not because of righteous things we had done, but because of his mercy." Paul here is noting the motivation behind God's decision to provide for our salvation. Both Catholics and Evangelicals agree that there is nothing in us that would cause God to save us. It was pure mercy that caused him to pour out his grace on us. This verse does not deal at all with the "how" of justification, either.

It also might be helpful for Evangelicals to know that Catholics do not believe that our works are innately valuable. The same could be said of our faith. If either is valuable to God, it is only because he graciously decided to make it so. They are meritorious only because by grace God has connected them to the work of Christ and the Cross. "Grace . . . ensures the supernatural quality of our acts and consequently their merit before God and before men" (CCC 2011). Even our ability to do works is a result of God's grace working through us. This is what Augustine meant when he said, "All our good merits are wrought through grace, so that God, in crowning our merits, is crowning nothing but his gifts." Our responsibility is to cooperate with God: "Do not put out the Spirit's fire" (1 Th 5:19).

While at Trinity, I became very close friends with Jim, a Catholic student at Loyola University. One day we were discussing salvation. I was attempting to lead him down the "Roman Road", a plan of salvation lifted from the Book of Romans. In exasperation, Jim finally asked me why I used only verses from Paul and never quoted verses from Jesus. At the time (twenty-five years ago), it struck me as odd to make that distinction, but there is an important point hidden in his comment.

Catholics unashamedly start with the Gospels and base their soteriology on Jesus' teachings. They look at all the rest of the New Testament as an expansion on Jesus, which must be understood in the light of his teachings.

Evangelicals start their study of soteriology with the Pauline epistles. They relegate all the rest of the Bible to being a footnote to Paul, including the teaching of Jesus. This may sound like a harsh generalization, but a check of the Evangelical literature bears this out.

This approach to Scripture bears an uncomfortably close

resemblance to the Marcionite heresy. Marcion was a second-century Gnostic who relegated most of the New Testament and all of the Old Testament to second-place status under ten Pauline epistles. He also taught that people of the Old Testament lived under an entirely different spiritual economy from people of the New Testament. (That will sound more than vaguely familiar to many Evangelicals, particularly dispensationalists and hyper-dispensationalists.) Because Marcion led the first major split in the Church, Polycarp (a disciple of the apostle John) called him "the firstborn of Satan". Thankfully, the heresy later exhausted itself.

Although there are substantive differences, because Marcion was a full-blown Gnostic and viciously anti-Semitic, Evangelicals exhibit a tendency toward Marcion's other errors. I cannot begin to count the number of times an Evangelical has dismissed a parable or saying of Jesus with, "Well, of course, that does not apply to us in the church age." Many Evangelicals would dismiss many of the verses cited earlier in this section, because they were the words of Jesus. They teach that very few, if any, of Jesus' teachings apply directly to Christians today: the people of Jesus' time lived under the law, whereas we live under grace. I know of one speaker, affiliated with Moody Bible Institute, who refused to speak on any book of the Bible outside of the Pauline epistles, because none of them applied to present-day Christians.

One of the early messianic prophecies in the Old Testament foretold that the Messiah would be a new "Moses" (Dt 18:15). Just as Moses founded the Old Testament, so the Messiah would found the New Testament. This was an important point to both Peter and Stephen, as they included it in their sermons: "For Moses said, 'The Lord your God will raise up for you a prophet like me from among your own people; you must listen to everything he tells you'" (Acts 3:22, 7:37).

What would Evangelicals think of any theologian who insisted on starting with the major and minor prophetic books of the Old Testament, developing a theology from them, and then squeezing the books of Moses into that mold? It would clearly be a case of putting the cart before the horse. Yet, that is precisely what Evangelicals have done with regard to Pauline soteriology and Jesus. Yes, we must understand Paul, but not in opposition to the gospel of Jesus.

When one starts with the gospel of Jesus, I believe it is inevitable that a Catholic view of salvation will be developed. We are saved by grace, justified by faith and works. Separate the faith from the works, and it dies. We can take no credit for our salvation, because both the faith and the works are a result of God's grace being operative in our lives. God has ordained that this is the method by which we merit salvation. He might have ordained a different way instead, but Scripture teaches us he did it this way.

This emphasis on justification by faith *and* works makes a tremendous practical difference. Ordinary Catholics tend to be less cerebral in their faith because the need for works involves more action. Evangelicals sometimes think of salvation as a kind of quiz. Get the right answer and you're in! They ask people, "When you die, and Jesus asks you at the gates of heaven, 'Why should I let you into my heaven?' What will you say?" What a question! Jesus nowhere implies that judgment will be a quiz in which the correct answer gets you in and the wrong one forces you out. Perhaps someone has been watching too many game shows on television. "Wheel of Fortune" has nothing to do with entering heaven. Entrance to heaven is preceded by a judgment: a judgment of what we have done in our lives. The criterion in every judgment scene in the New Testament is *works*: "Not everyone who says to me, 'Lord, Lord,' will enter the kingdom of heaven, but only he who *does* the will of my Father" (Mt 7:21; see also Jn 5, Mt 23, Rev 22, and 1 Cor 3).

As a youngster, if I had some extra time and I wanted to please God, I would read my Bible. Because of the Evangelical emphasis on faith and the mind, reading the Bible made perfect sense. The only sure way for God to reach you was through your mind. Making sure that what you believed was correct was the only sure way for you to reach God.

Because Catholic theology makes the will the predominant aspect of the soul, obedience through works takes on more importance. A Catholic youngster may not have all the right answers at the tip of his tongue, but he should have been taught to help someone in need. At the judgment Jesus will then say, "I tell you the truth, whatever you did for one of the least of these brothers of mine, you did for me" (Mt 25:40).

The emphasis on continual justification by "graceful works" also affects our view of conversion. Evangelicals make certain that they experience a conversion at some point in their lives. For the rest of their lives they will point back to that conversion as the day they were "born again", or "saved". Their eternal destiny is secured.

Catholics believes in an initial conversion but also that we must continually be converted. For Catholics, if it has been more than a few minutes since we repented and converted, it has probably been too long. The sacrament of Penance (reconciliation or confession) is an opportunity for continued conversion.

This is not to say that there may not come major turning points in a Catholic's Christian commitment. Francis of Assisi had a major conversion at the beginning of his adulthood. He was, however, already a Christian. He continued to have daily conversions throughout the rest of his life. Thomas

Aquinas wrote and lectured on Christian theology his whole life. He was a Christian of towering intellect, faith, and spirituality. Yet, toward the end of his life he had a major conversion. From the Catholic perspective, a conversion occurs any time we choose God over self. This must be a regular event, but occasionally it is an event that changes the entire direction of our lives.

So what role do works play in our justification? They put faith into concrete, physical action. We are not like fallen angels. Because angels do not have physical bodies, when they fell they were instantly and thoroughly damnable. But we have bodies linked to our spirits. We can desire something at the spiritual level of our beings but fail to accomplish it at the physical level. The role of works is to develop our characters (souls, wills) so that the physical side of us is eventually made to be in harmony with our spiritual desires. This can take a lifetime. In the process, we expand our character in order to become more Christlike. Our faith does not just cover up our rebellious wills so that we can slip into heaven. Our faith makes us want to work at reforming ourselves into Christ's image. When we are "perfect as our heavenly Father is perfect" (Mt 5:48), then we are ready for heaven.

Do we have any indication that our character does in fact need purification even after our sins are forgiven? Are Catholics right when they claim that even after our guilt is forgiven the effect of sin remains on our wills? Does sin not only damage our relationship with God but also deform our very souls?

Think about the first time a person commits a particular sin. Take lying as an example. If the person has never told an untruth before and has been trained properly, telling a lie will be a very difficult experience. Everything in that person's character and conscience will revolt at this first lie. That is less true of the second lie. The third lie is even easier for this person. By the tenth lie, the conscience and character of this person hardly flinch at sin. Why?

This change occurs because, not only does a sin offend God, it gradually destroys the person who sins. Every time another lie is told, a small imperfection, or wart, or crack is made on the liar's character. Confession and God's forgiveness can and do take care of the offense toward God, but the liar's character is still damaged. Can we be sure of this? Yes. Even after this person has been forgiven, it is easier for him to lie than it was before he ever told his first lie. He has developed a bad habit. His soul itself has an imperfection.

That is the role of works in our justification. Works mold our character over time. They slowly erase the imperfections, warts, and cracks that make it easier for us to sin again. Over a lifetime, they enable us to become more like Christ. When we are finally Christlike, we are ready for heaven.

This truth protects us from indulging in the sin of presumption. Presumption can be a real problem in Evangelical circles. The president of one prominent seminary has publicly bemoaned the fact that so few elderly Evangelicals are living out their faith. Evangelicalism galvanizes the young but not the old. Perhaps a deficient theology of salvation is to blame.

Catholics speak of heaven as our *hope*. Evangelicals prefer to speak of *knowing* that one is saved. Although Scripture uses both terminologies, actually Catholics are using the more common biblical language. Faith, hope, and charity are the three virtues of 1 Corinthians 13:13. Our hope is in Christ and his promise of heaven: "We wait eagerly for our adoption as sons, the redemption of our bodies. For in this *hope* we were saved. But *hope* that is seen is not *hope* at all. Who *hopes* for what he already has? But if we *hope* for what we do not yet have, we wait for it patiently" (Rom 8:23–25). Catholic literature describes our hope as a "certain confidence".

When asked if he was going to heaven, one pope replied, "I hope so." He has been roundly criticized by Evangelicals. Yet it is a perfectly biblical response.

This brings us to another communication misunderstanding between Catholics and Evangelicals. When a Catholic dies, and an Evangelical inquires about his prospects for heaven, it is common for a Catholic to say, "Oh, I'm sure he is in heaven. He was such a good man." This statement drives Evangelicals to distraction, convincing them that the dead Catholic had no chance at heaven at all! The presuppositions behind the statement seem to fly in the face of everything that Evangelicals believe. Because the Evangelical sees no place for works in justification, he wants to hear that the dead Catholic had placed his faith in Christ alone.

The Catholic, however, is not stating his convictions with theological precision. If he were, or if he could, he would state the situation something like this: "Our friend was baptized into the body of Christ. His faith in Christ was clearly evidenced by his life of good works. I know of no unrepented serious sin in his life, so I believe he will spend eternity with God." This would be a more accurate way to state the Catholic position, but who has the presence of mind to say that at a funeral? Evangelicals should understand that the Catholic position regarding faith and works is a teaching of the Bible and worry less about how it is phrased.

So far we have seen that sinning makes it easier to sin again. This is because sin harms the soul. We also know that sin creates guilt with God. Catholics and Evangelicals agree on this. God forgives us of our guilt based on the merits of Christ's work on the Cross. But Catholics discern a third effect of sin: the need for satisfaction of the temporal punishment for sin. This is different from the guilt punishable by eternal damnation. Catholics call this satisfaction "expiation".

The existence of temporal punishment, as distinct from our eternal punishment and forgiveness, is very clear in Scripture. David was forgiven of the guilt of his adultery, but his baby died and havoc continued to reign in his family. This was temporal punishment for his already forgiven guilt (2 Sam 12:11–14). Moses was forgiven for striking the rock a second time, against God's specific instructions. His eternal destiny was still secure, but he was refused entry into the Promised Land as temporal punishment (Nb 20:12, Dt 34:4).

There are several ways for the Christian to expiate the temporal punishment remaining even after his eternal guilt is forgiven. Suffering in this world is one of these ways. In college I read *The Problem of Pain*, by C. S. Lewis, for the first time. It made tremendous sense to me. His major point is that suffering is not random, and it can even be good. Suffering helps a Christian grow even when no one else knows about it. Suffering teaches unqualified obedience. This perspective is good, but incomplete.

When I read the writings of Pope John Paul II, I encountered a deeper meaning of suffering, one that is solidly biblical. Not only does suffering perfect me in obedience, it is integral to my salvation. Although suffering is never enjoyable, this concept infuses suffering with dignity. Suffering purifies us in our pilgrimage toward heaven. "Although he was a son, he learned obedience from what he suffered and, once made perfect, he became the source of eternal salvation for all who obey him" (Heb 5:8–9). When we are perfected, we are ready for the presence of God.

In Catholic literature on suffering, I discovered a depth of spirituality I never even dreamed was available in print. To use a current slang expression, this literature is "awesome".

Jesus certainly minced no words when it came to our need for suffering. He called it the cross. "Anyone who does not take his cross and follow me is not worthy of me" (Mt 10:38). "If anyone would come after me, he must deny himself and take up his cross and follow me" (Mt 16:24). To have our feet in the footprints of Jesus, our backs must bear a cross.

The exciting thing is that, in some mysterious way, our suffering can even help other people's salvation. "Now I rejoice in what was suffered for you, and *I fill up in my flesh what is still lacking in regard to Christ's afflictions*, for the sake of his body, which is the church" (Col 1:24). Paul writes here that his suffering for the Colossians actually fills up what was lacking in Christ's afflictions.

An Evangelical is hard pressed to find any meaning to the words "what is still lacking in . . . Christ's afflictions" without emptying the verse of all meaning. Taken seriously, this verse destroys Evangelical soteriology. Evangelicals state without reservation that nothing we do can further our salvation (or anyone else's). Faith alone justifies, not works or suffering. Yet this verse contradicts that view of salvation. (There are other instances in Scripture that lend credence to the teaching that one person can do something to help in the salvation of another. The principle is enunciated starting as far back as Job 1:5.)

Pope John Paul II expressed the teaching of the Church on this verse and on suffering in his encyclical *Salvifici doloris*. This is a long passage but well worth pondering:

> In the Paschal Mystery Christ began the union with men in the community of the Church. The mystery of the Church is expressed in this: . . . the Church is continually being built up spiritually as the Body of Christ. In this

Body, Christ wishes to be united with every individual, and in a special way He is united to those who suffer. . . . The sufferings of Christ created the good of the world's Redemption. This good in itself is inexhaustible and infinite. No man can add anything to it. But at the same time, in the mystery of the Church as His Body, Christ has in a sense opened His own redemptive suffering to all human suffering. Insofar as man becomes a sharer in Christ's sufferings . . . to that extent he in his own way completes the suffering through which Christ accomplished the Redemption of the world. Does this mean that the Redemption achieved by Christ is not complete? No. It only means that the Redemption, accomplished through satisfactory love, remains always open to all love expressed in human suffering. . . . Christ achieved the Redemption completely and to the very limit; but at the same time He did not bring it to a close. . . . It seems to be part of the very essence of Christ's redemptive suffering that this suffering requires to be unceasingly completed.

The fact that Evangelicals are uncomfortable with this concept does not change the fact that it is based solidly in Scripture. My suffering can further the salvation of others as well as my own. Suffering in the present helps in the application of the graces won for us by Christ on the Cross. By offering up my suffering in union with Christ's, I raise my suffering to a new level of significance. Suffering becomes holy.

This role of work and suffering in our salvation is clear in Scripture. Perhaps this is the gateway through which Evangelicals can understand two Catholic doctrines that are not so clearly taught in Scripture. (That is not to say they are not in harmony with Scripture. They are a part of that original oral tradition of the Church that Paul referred to in his writings to Timothy.) We can see these two dogmas as assumptions behind verses in Scripture, even though they never needed direct teaching. I have mentioned them already. The two dogmas I am referring to are indulgences and purgatory.

Indulgences were the hardest issue for me to resolve in my reconciliation with Catholicism. For that reason, it was one of the last with which I made peace. I finally followed the example of G. K. Chesterton. He struggled with a different teaching of the Church: the discipline of celibate priests and virgin nuns in the Church. That just made no sense to him. He finally accepted it because it had been a part of the Church for her entire history. He concluded that if all the thinkers throughout all that time had found celibacy necessary and reasonable, then the problem was most likely with him, not with the Church. It seemed more probable to him that he was being influenced by something in his culture or upbringing or temperament than that all the saints, throughout almost twenty centuries, had been wrong. He still felt uncomfortable with celibacy, but his will submitted to the wisdom of the Church throughout the ages, and he accepted the teaching.

This is a fair description of my experience with indulgences. My American cultural background was working against me whenever I pondered this doctrine. We are taught to value our independence, but indulgences are rooted in the concept of our spiritual interdependence. They make sense only within the biblical teaching of the body of Christ and the communion of the saints. We are spiritually interdependent. Yet that concept grates on American individualism. My American culture was causing a spiritual blind spot.

As an Evangelical, I found it easy to think of the United States as the most important part of the church, the place on earth where we saw truth most objectively. The issue of indulgences reminded me that such was not the case. Just as the early, sophisticated church in Corinth had to submit to the backwater, unrefined Church in Rome, so did I in Chicago.

Before I could overcome the obstacles, however, my first step was to learn what indulgences actually are. An indulgence is one more way of satisfying the need for temporal punishment (we have already looked at suffering). They are *not* a method of obtaining forgiveness for the guilt of our sins. That must be accomplished through repentance, which is available based on the finished work of Christ.

When a Catholic receives an indulgence, a portion, or all, of his temporal punishment is expiated. An indulgence consists most commonly of an act of worship or prayer. Occasionally an indulgence will require a contribution to some need, along with a specific act of worship or prayer. Never has the Church taught that a simple contribution of money is sufficient to acquire an indulgence. The soul of the sinner must be repentant and worshipful.

The whole concept of indulgences is grounded on the role of works and suffering in the perfection of our souls. The Church is the repository of the graces earned by Christ and those sufferings of the saints mentioned by Paul (Jn 20:22–23; Mt 16:13–20). This pool of grace is infinite. As such, the Church has the power to dispense graces to needy Christians endeavoring to purify their souls.

Evangelicals are fond of saying that God has no grandchildren. They mean that each of us must respond personally to God's call. That is certainly true. But it does not necessarily follow that Christians are orphans, with no siblings and no family. God gives us a family, the Church, to help us in our pilgrimage to holiness. Indulgences are one of those helps.

This belief of the Church was evident with the very earliest of the Christian martyrs. When a sinner of the early

Church confessed his sin, he might have been given a very lengthy penance, or time of purification through effort. These early sinners quite often went to visit the (soon to be) martyrs in prison and were "lent" by them some of their merits with God, merits that had been accrued through suffering and a holy life. When the sinner returned to his bishop, his penance could be declared satisfied, based on the martyr's merits. Let me reiterate, this did not affect the sinner's eternal guilt but only his temporal punishment.

The whole concept is very foreign to Evangelicals, but I could not discern anything essentially unbiblical in it. That is not to say that it does not contradict Evangelical notions of salvation. But I could not deny that the practice of indulgences dated from the very earliest of the Christian communities. As did Chesterton, I submitted my will in spite of my emotions.

Perhaps I should add that most Catholics agree that Luther was correct in his attack on the abuses of indulgences occurring during his time. A good many bishops had been fighting those same abuses for years before Luther condemned them. But the abuse of something does not invalidate its proper practice for all time. The abuse should be corrected so that the thing can be properly used. No need to throw out the baby with the bath water.

Personally, purgatory made much more sense right from the start, but it is not understood at all by most Evangelicals. The word itself is enough to make the heart of many Evangelicals skip a beat. My son told me he had been told by a teacher that Catholics believe purgatory is just like hell, only not quite as bad. After researching Catholic teaching itself, I find myself asking, "Where *do* Evangelicals come up with this stuff?"

There are three places for the dead. Hell is a permanent

place of suffering and unhappiness. Once there, no one leaves. Heaven is a permanent place of comfort and happiness. Once there, no one would want to leave. Purgatory is a temporary place of suffering and unhappiness. Actually, purgatory is the entranceway to heaven. It is not a second chance at heaven. It is temporary because only those people assured of heaven enter purgatory. The souls in purgatory are essentially happy because they know their eternal destiny is secure.

Why is purgatory necessary? Jesus said that "the pure in heart . . . will see God" (Mt 5:8). Only those Christians with pure souls can see God. God uses our daily Christian lives to purify us and prepare us to see him. Only when we are pure, really pure on the inside, will we see God. We have Jesus' word on that.

Many Christians, Evangelicals included, may be that pure when they die. They go directly to heaven. But what of the Christian who has not allowed God to purify him completely of the effects of sin on his character during his earthly lifetime? His guilt has been forgiven, but the imperfections, warts, and cracks on his soul remain. His temporal punishment has not been expiated.

That is the purpose of purgatory. It is a temporary place where souls that are not completely pure through work and suffering here on earth can become pure through temporary suffering after death. When a soul is pure, it enters heaven. Purgatory is far from being a terrible doctrine; it is a comfort to know there is a place to complete the work on my character begun here on earth.

When we first investigated this doctrine as a family, one of my sons asked, "If only the pure in heart see God, why couldn't there be two parts to heaven? One for those who can see God—the pure—and one for those who can't—the less than perfectly pure." I thought about that much of the night.

The next day I told him that he had it exactly right (though soon I would add a qualification). Purgatory is like the entrance or vestibule to heaven. Purgatory will cease to exist when the last soul has been "purged", and all heaven will see God.

Belief in purgatory is evident in the very earliest years of Christianity. It seems likely that it was never mentioned in Scripture for the simple fact that the teaching was never questioned. Augustine, in *The City of God*, said, "Temporal punishments are suffered by some in this life only, by others after death, by others both now and then." This is clearly a reference to purgatory.

Purgatory is the only way to make sense out of prayers for the dead. Our prayers help them in their suffering to become pure enough for heaven. Prayers for the dead are contained in the very early Christian writings. In 2 Maccabees 12:43–46, prayers and offerings are given for the benefit of those already dead: "It is a holy and wholesome thought to pray for the dead, that they might be loosed from their sins." The loosing obviously occurs in purgatory.

Although the exact meaning of 1 Corinthians 15:29 is hotly debated, one fact is quite clear. Living Christians can do something to benefit those souls already dead: "Now if there is no resurrection, what will those do who are baptized for the dead? If the dead are not raised at all, why are people baptized for them?" This verse makes absolutely no sense within the Evangelical concept of heaven and hell. Without purgatory, what could possibly be gained by doing anything for the dead? Their destiny is unalterable. The uninterrupted teaching of the Church has been that our prayers do benefit dead Christians.

Other verses that make more sense within the context of a belief in purgatory are scattered throughout Scripture. In

Matthew 12:32, Jesus implies that some sins can be cleared from our account here and some in the afterlife: "Anyone who speaks against the Holy Spirit will not be forgiven, either in this age or in the age to come." Purgatory makes the most sense of this verse. Without purgatory, the last portion of Jesus' statement seems frivolous.

The verse 1 Corinthians 3:15 fits in precisely with the Catholic dogma of purgatory, but it makes less sense with an Evangelical soteriology: "If it [each man's work] is burned up, he will suffer loss; he himself will be saved, but only as one escaping through the flames."

In Hebrews 12:23 we see several groups of people mentioned. Interestingly, there is a distinction made between the "the church of the firstborn" and those "righteous men made perfect". This dovetails nicely with the Church's teaching concerning purgatory. There is a reference to those who die and go directly to heaven ("firstborn") versus those who must undergo the purification process of purgatory ("made perfect").

In the parable told by Jesus in Luke 12:42–48, there are three types of servants, who are treated in three different ways. It "will be good" for the "faithful and wise manager" (heaven). The servant "who knows" but "does not do what his master wants" will be put into a "place with the unbelievers" (hell). Finally, the servant who "does things deserving of punishment" but "does not know" will be disciplined (purgatory).

Although the Bible never mentions the word "purgatory", it does make clear that there is a third place besides heaven and hell: "For Christ . . . went and preached to the spirits in prison who disobeyed long ago" (1 Pet 3:18–20). Because the authority of the Church teaches that the third place is purgatory, that is the name I use, as well.

There is another issue of soteriology on which Evangelicals and Catholics disagree. It relates to how one starts on this pilgrimage called the Christian life. For Evangelicals, the pilgrimage starts as the result of a conscious decision to put one's faith solely in Christ's work on the Cross. That act of belief makes one a Christian and assures one of heaven. Only then is one baptized, usually as a teenager or adult. The act of baptism is merely a proclamation that the sinner is now a Christian endeavoring to follow Christ.

Let me remind the reader that there are three major evangelical views of baptism. I will attend to only one of them. In the first section I defined how I would use the word "Evangelical". Most of these people attend Baptist churches, Community churches, Bible churches, Evangelical Free churches, and so forth.

All three evangelical views of baptism leave a gaping ache in the heart for all those who have died before hearing the gospel, either as infants or pagans. Perhaps this is best illustrated by the various Protestant and Catholic burial practices in colonial America. When a Catholic infant died, he was given a Christian burial in the church graveyard. Within certain communities, when a Protestant infant died, he was buried with only a civil (non-Christian) ceremony in burial plots reserved for the heathen. The Protestant child could not be considered fully Christian by his community until he reached the age of reason and he himself had made a commitment to Christ.

For Catholics, the Christian pilgrimage starts at baptism, usually as an infant. As we have seen, however, from a Catholic perspective the journey is much more complex after its beginning. It is a gross inaccuracy to say that Catholics believe we are saved by baptism. Baptism is only the means God uses initially to infuse grace. Grace works in us to save us. Is there biblical evidence for the Catholic teaching concerning baptism?

Actually, the evidence in favor of the belief that water baptism starts the process of salvation is rather overwhelming in the Bible. It is only by bringing to the Scripture a virulent anti-physical bias that the evidence can be avoided. This common Evangelical prejudice can be stated like this: "Nothing we do with our bodies in the physical realm has anything whatsoever to do with God's dealings with our eternal souls in the spiritual realm."

The people of the early Church did not share this bias. Julian the Apostate was baptized and raised a Christian in the mid-fourth century. As an adult, he wanted to undo his commitment to Christianity. It would never be enough just to state that he did not choose to be Christian any longer; he knew he needed to do something physical. He was not a bodiless angel; he was a man with a body and a soul. So he was baptized in the blood of bulls in order to undo his Christian baptism. That must have been a horrible mess, but it illustrates how firmly the ancient Church believed in the union of the spiritual and the physical.

Actually, the anti-physical bias is nothing new. Its origin is in a Gnostic heresy called Manicheaism. We have already seen the effect of this bias on Evangelical views of the Eucharist. Although Scripture clearly teaches that physical substances do impart spiritual benefits, grace (John 6:26–59), Evangelicals stick by their prejudice. This notion that we should worship like angels, without the aid of our bodies, leads Evangelicals to reject other things besides the Eucharist and baptism. I have come to believe that this bias distorts the Evangelical understanding of baptism, marriage, death, Communion, the body of Christ, grace, Mary, the Holy Spirit, and even the Incarnation.

Largely to accommodate this bias, Evangelicals redefine the meaning of baptism in Scripture. All lexicographers agree the word literally means the physical immersion of something. Ancient Jewish writers used it this way, to describe physical immersion in water. From the very start, Christian use of the term has meant a use of water with the participation of the Holy Spirit. Evangelicals redefine the word baptism to mean a spiritual immersion of the Holy Spirit alone, with water not even involved. They do this without adequate scriptural basis and without early Church precedent.

If we simply come to Scripture without this bias and understand baptism in its usual meaning of immersion in water, we see that the Bible teaches that the Spirit of God uses the physical act to impart his grace to us. Unless one comes to the passage with an unshakable anti-physical prejudice already in place, the text of Scripture speaks for itself. One is left with the firm impression that Catholics are right. If baptism is administered correctly, grace is transmitted to the newly baptized by God's Spirit: *ex opere operato*.

It is through physical baptism that God initially grants us forgiveness of sins. The word-picture that Paul paints in his Jerusalem sermon is unmistakable. Paul describes a physical action with spiritual consequences: "What are you waiting for? Get up, be baptized and wash your sins away, calling on his name" (Acts 22:16).

The fact that physical baptism is the moment when the Holy Spirit becomes operative in one's life is quite clear. Peter, under the inspiration of the Holy Spirit, preached, "Repent and be baptized . . . and you will receive the gift of the Holy Spirit" (Acts 2:38).

In 1 Corinthians 12:13, we learn that baptism grants us membership in the Church, the body of Christ: "For we were all baptized by one Spirit into one body." This is actually a union with Christ that makes God our Father and entitles us to the riches of heaven: "For all of you who were baptized into Christ have been clothed with Christ . . . since you are a son, God has made you also an heir" (Gal 3:26–4:7).

We participate in the death of Christ through baptism. Our resurrection to new life occurs on coming up from the water so that we can live here on this earth, in real, physical bodies, to the glory of God: "We were therefore buried with him through baptism into death in order that, just as Christ was raised from the dead through the glory of the Father, we too may live a new life" (Rom 6:4; see Col 2:12).

To sum it all up, we could say that baptism is the starting point of our salvation: "This water [of the flood] symbolizes the baptism that now saves you also—not the removal of dirt from the body. . . . It saves you by the resurrection of Jesus Christ" (1 Pet 3:21).

The major scriptural objection raised concerning the necessity of physical baptism for regeneration is primarily that sometimes in Scripture baptism is not mentioned along with faith. I had always been taught that this proved that faith alone was sufficient and that baptism was superfluous. This bothered me, however. It just did not ring true. The verses that mention baptism are so strong and clear. The argument against the necessity of baptism is primarily an argument from silence, the weakest type of argument. If baptism is not necessary, then the verses I have mentioned above (and more) are very difficult to interpret indeed.

I came to the solution one day while ordering a hot dog. I saw that the vendor would need to know my tastes concerning mustard, pickle, relish, tomato, catsup, peppers, chili, french fries, and sauerkraut. What he would never do, though, was ask me about the bun. If I requested a hot dog, he would assume that I wanted a hot dog on a bun. The bun was understood. Ordering a "hot dog" had come to be a shorthand way of ordering a "hot dog on a bun".

Then I saw that the same mechanism had been at work in the early Church concerning baptism. The proper way to describe one's entry into Christianity was "Repent and be baptized" (Acts 2:38). This is clear from the very beginning, with Peter's first sermon. At the time of that sermon, those in the crowd had no idea what was expected of them. Baptism was integral to the process of becoming a Christian, as so many verses point out.

As time went on, it became common knowledge that anyone who believed would also be baptized. Paul's admonition to the Philippian jailer, "Believe on the Lord Jesus Christ", was a shorthand way of saying "believe and be baptized". Paul had been preaching in Philippi for some time. The gospel message had become better known throughout the Roman world. Belief had become an enriched term, meaning much more than merely mental assent. It was understood that anyone who truly believed would repent and take the step of baptism in order to be "baptized by one Spirit into [the] one body" (1 Cor 12:13).

This shorthand way of talking is such an everyday part of our lives that we do not see it unless we stop to think about it. It struck me as the most true-to-life way to harmonize the verses that clearly declare baptism a necessary part of becoming a Christian with those that merely omit it.

No longer did I need to explain away the statement of Jesus to Nicodemus, "Unless a man is born of water and the Spirit, he cannot enter the kingdom of God" (Jn 3:5). Water baptism is used by the Holy Spirit to regenerate us.

One last miscommunication between Catholics and Evangelicals needs to be explored. When Evangelicals talk about Christianity, they almost always discuss it in terms of a "personal relationship" with God. For some reason, they think that Catholics do not believe in having a personal relationship with God.

Actually, the Church does speak in this manner. The *Catechism of the Catholic Church* clearly states, "The mystery of the faith . . . requires that the faithful . . . live . . . in a vital and personal relationship with the living and true God" (CCC 2558). When one of my sons was preparing for his First Communion, he was taught a prayer referring to the personal relationship he had with Christ. The prayer also spoke of receiving Christ into his heart and life.

While the Church obviously believes that a personal relationship is a helpful concept in today's culture, Catholics are not in danger of viewing this as the only essential way of expressing Christian faith. Some Evangelicals are. One major Evangelical denomination has stated recently that although it will cooperate with Catholic organizations on moral issues, it will still actively seek to convert individual Catholics who are "without a personal relationship with Christ".

Twentieth-century America is so self-absorbed, even narcissistic, that we find it difficult to imagine a culture devoid of our level of self-consciousness. In our culture we may find it helpful to describe Christianity as having "a personal relationship with God", but we should not assume that the members of the early Church also found that a helpful way to describe their faith. The expression is never used in Scripture. It is a product of our present cultural way of thinking. A more biblical expression is "following Christ".

My point is this: Evangelicals must not assume that because a Catholic is unfamiliar with their language he is somehow less of a Christian. There are good biblical reasons with long historical precedent for the way Catholics express themselves.

Dr. Lovelace is an evangelical at Gordon Conwell Seminary who has studied past American revivals (awakenings). He writes that "unity and renewal go hand in hand" and "Every Awakening brought a convergence of the Catholic and Protestant traditions." Many Evangelicals do desire a revival for America in our generation. Perhaps if Evangelicals buried the hatchet with their Catholic brethren, we would all be one step closer to experiencing another awakening.

At the end of my investigation into Catholic soteriology, I found myself buying into an entire systematic theology as I had never been able to do before. Since beginning seminary I had looked for, but had never been able to find, a systematic theology that dealt with all the data of Scripture. Every single one had fudged certain verses or ignored others in order to make its system work. This had bothered me immensely. At last I discovered one that did not have to do this. Catholicism incorporates all of Scripture in its thought. That makes perfect sense when one finally understands that Catholics, with Catholic theological assumptions, wrote the Bible.

VIII

The Incarnation

The average practicing Catholic's goal is regularly to spend about fifteen minutes meditating on the events and meaning of the Incarnation. Many do this every day, while others do it once a week. Many Catholic families spend this meditation time together on Sunday. In addition, many Catholics make a habit of praying, three times a day, a short prayer that focuses their minds and hearts on the Incarnation. This means that the historical events of the Incarnation are the heart and soul of everyday Catholic devotion.

It would probably come as a surprise to most Catholics that the average Evangelical would not even think of meditating on the meaning of the Incarnation for fifteen minutes a week, or a month, or even fifteen minutes a year. At best, he would meditate on its meaning when he read the Gospels in his devotions. This might happen once a year, or once a decade. Why this difference in priorities?

Although most Evangelicals will not agree with my conclusion, I think the evidence supports it: Evangelicals are uncomfortable with the implications of the Incarnation. Whenever we are uncomfortable with something, we tend to neglect or ignore it. That is the reaction of many Evangelicals. They accept the Incarnation, believe in it firmly as an orthodox dogma, but do not delve into its implications. If they did, they would find themselves entertaining conclusions they find objectionable.

One implication of the Incarnation is that God loved our bodies enough to take one himself. In eternity we will not shed our bodies; rather, we will have them "enhanced". "The Lord Jesus Christ . . . will transform our lowly bodies, so that they will be like his glorious body" (Phil 3:20). God loves bodily form enough to give us a new and improved model when ours dies. We might say that heaven is not complete without physical bodies worshipping God.

Another implication of the Incarnation is that it took a physical act on the part of God himself to cure our spiritual problem. We are not told why, but our spiritual rebellion required physical solutions. This has always been true. When Adam sinned, God caused an animal to be killed. All through the Old Covenant, a sin against God required a physical atonement. At the Incarnation, heaven staged an invasion of our physical earth. In the New Covenant, the physical aspect of the sacrifice is imparted with new significance. The physical body of the victim is now that of the God-man, Jesus.

The physical mission of the Incarnation continues today in the Church. The Church is the mystical body of Christ. This is a favorite theme of Paul. The Church's soul is divine, namely, the indwelling Holy Spirit. As with the God-man, the Church has her human element as well. The Church continues the work of God that Jesus initiated in his Incarnation: the salvation of the world. It does not happen outside the physical realm. The continued invasion of earth by heaven, begun in the Incarnation, will continue within our physical surroundings.

Tom Howard points out, in *Evangelical Is Not Enough*, that evangelicals have a bias against the physical. This prejudice is reminiscent of the Manicheans, Gnostic heretics of the early Church. Many Evangelicals are firmly convinced that God does not utilize the physical to interact with us spiritually. We have already discussed how this bias limits the Evangelical ability to appreciate the Eucharist and baptism as they are taught in Scripture. There are other areas affected by this prejudice against the physical.

The most obvious entails how we worship. If God loves our bodies, we should respond by using them to worship him. When Catholics enter the church for worship, they stop at the holy water receptacle by the door. They dip their finger in the water and make the sign of the cross over themselves. They touch their forehead, then their chest, then each of their shoulders. The water reminds them of their baptism. By simultaneously praying "In the name of the Father, and of the Son, and of the Holy Spirit, Amen", they remind themselves of the Trinity. The sign of the cross reminds them of what it cost to grant them redemption. It reminds them that they are called to carry a cross daily as well.

On reaching their pews, they genuflect (lower themselves onto one knee) in the direction of the tabernacle. This is a sign of respect, similar to the way one treats royalty. Christ is royalty of the highest order. The tabernacle is where Christ dwells, body, soul, and divinity. A special candle is alight near the tabernacle so all will know that Christ is physically present in the church. On reaching their seats, Catholics will kneel, cross themselves again, and pray. During this time it is common for them to collect themselves, examine their consciences, and begin to worship. This allows time for God to speak to their consciences concerning the previous week and for them to give him thanks for all his gifts. In the front of the church is the altar, where the eucharistic sacrifice will occur.

As the Mass begins, the congregation will sit during certain portions, such as when the minister is preaching. They will stand out of respect during certain portions, such as when the Gospel is read. Finally, they will kneel in worship (cf. Neh 8:6) during certain portions, such as during the central prayer, when Christ becomes physically present in the communion elements during the Consecration. When they leave, they will again genuflect on one knee and use the water to make the sign of the cross as they exit.

All these actions strike the Evangelical as strange. Because they are unfamiliar, the description that comes to mind for most Evangelicals is "ritualistic" or "superstitious". I know, because that is exactly what I thought for most of my life.

But we should never judge something we do not understand. Catholics worship God with their whole bodies. They do this because we are not angels. Angels have no bodies. If they did, do we really think they would refuse to humble their bodies by kneeling in reverence?

Revelation portrays heaven as a place where angels and redeemed people worship in holy awe: "The twenty-four elders fall down before him who sits on the throne, and worship him" (Rev 4:9–11). The elders use their bodies to worship. Dare we do less with our physical bodies here on earth?

Catholics enjoy using every sense in their worship. When my family and I became Catholics, we already knew how to use our ears and voices to worship God. Evangelicals sing better than almost anyone else. I have found the music at some Catholic churches to be better than others. I love to sing. When I sing in a Catholic service, it is easier for me to keep my eyes on Christ and my mind on the words. I appreciate the absence of a leader in the front of the church waving his arms and, between verses, telling me to sing louder.

Incense is used, as it was in the Old Testament, to symbolize prayer ascending to God. It can also remind us of where we are and why: God is there to be worshipped. My wife uses perfume to much the same purpose: it is a reminder to me of her presence. I have never faulted her for it.

Even taste and touch are used to worship God every Sunday. I taste the Body and Blood of Christ. I believe it is Christ's Body on the authority of his own words. Scripture is so clear on this point that only an overwhelming anti-physical bias can explain Evangelical teaching concerning the Eucharist. I touch his real Body in the Eucharist, and I touch his mystical body when I share his peace with my fellow worshippers. (This is a time during the Mass when the people greet one another with words such as "The peace of Christ be with you.") Even the disciples themselves never were closer to Christ in a real, physical way than I am at every Mass.

We have eyes, and Catholics want them to remind us of God and his redemptive work. The altar in almost every Catholic church has a crucifix (cross) on or above it. My local church happens to have a beautiful cast bronze statue of Christ on the Cross. I would guess it to be about seven feet tall. An Evangelical minister suggested this was because Catholics do not really believe in the Resurrection! I would have laughed, if the stakes had not been so high. When I look at that crucifix, my eyes help my soul to concentrate on what it took God to bring me into his Church. Catholics believe in the Resurrection, but there is no Easter without a Good Friday.

At first, the statues and the stained glass were a stumbling block for Colleen and me. This is not uncommon. (An Evangelical pastor shared that he cannot help laughing at dashboard statues of Mary in the cars of Catholics.) Once Colleen and I absorbed their purpose, though, statues became our helpers. We could direct our attention to the crucifix over the altar and know God understands that our intention is to worship him. In an Evangelical church, it is usually the pulpit, the preacher, or the choir that is the predominant feature in the front of the church. That arrangement makes it much harder to direct worship to God alone. All those people can get in the way.

There was a time when I would have brought up one of the Ten Commandments as an argument against images in church: "You shall not make for yourself an idol in the form of anything in heaven above or on the earth beneath or in the waters below. You shall not bow down to them or worship them" (Ex 20:4–5).

But Evangelicals fail to account for Exodus 25:18–22 and 36:8–35, where Moses is specifically commanded by God to make images for use in worshipping him. In Numbers 21:8–9, God commands Moses to make a bronze serpent in order to save those bitten by venomous serpents. A person who had been bitten had to see physically the image of the serpent in order to be healed. God commands the making of images again in 1 Kings 6:23–29 and 7:23–26, when Solomon builds the temple. Evidently the Ten Commandments prohibit the use of images when they are not connected to the worship of Yahweh. Catholic use of images fits in precisely with a biblical understanding of the Ten Commandments.

Evangelicals also use statues and images. For example, many Evangelicals use a crèche at Christmas time. It would be silly to accuse them of worshipping the figurine of the baby Jesus. Neither Catholics nor Evangelicals break any of the Ten Commandments by their use of images.

This brings us to another misunderstanding that is based on a different use of language. Catholics do not "worship" pictures, statues, and relics in the sense with which Evangelicals use the word "worship". That is evident in Catholic literature. Catholics use physical reminders to focus their souls on worship of God. God alone must be the ultimate object of all worship.

But there is another meaning of the word "worship" that is no longer in common usage. Before people started writing their own wedding vows, a bride promised to "obey" her new husband; a groom promised to "worship" his wife's body. The groom's vow did not entail idolatry. His promise was to respect her body as that place where new life is created. The meaning of worship in this context is "highly honor". In some older literature, the word "worship" was used in this sense; now we use the word "venerate", which is clearer.

Catholics speak of venerating images, the saints, or Mary. Catholic literature clearly teaches that it is a serious sin to worship anyone or anything other than God. Furthermore, whereas Evangelicals "worship", Catholics "worship", "adore", and "venerate". Catholics *worship* and *adore* God alone. They *venerate* Mary and the other saints and sacred images. "The honor paid to sacred images is a 'respectful veneration,' not the adoration due to God alone" (CCC 2132).

I always knew that the worship of the Old Covenant was a very physical ordeal. There were sheep, goats, doves, flames, knives, blood, and hooks. Yet, at that point, God the Son had not taken on a permanent physical body himself. Does it seem logical that God himself would enter the physical realm, only to ask us never to use our own bodies in worship? It seems implausible to me. Especially when I consider Scripture.

God loves our bodies and has a plan for them. "The Lord Jesus Christ . . . by the power that enables him to bring everything under his control, will transform our lowly bodies, so that they will be like his glorious body" (Phil 3:20). Paul tells us that he literally groans in anticipation of the time when his body will be redeemed: "We . . . groan inwardly as we wait eagerly for our adoption as sons, the *redemption of our bodies*" (Rom 8:20).

Hebrews specifically exhorts us to approach God with a sincere heart and a pure body. Both are necessary: "Let us draw near to God with a sincere heart . . . and having our bodies washed with pure water" (Heb 10:22). This should not surprise us when we remember that our bodies, not just our souls, are members of Christ's mystical body itself: "Do you not know that *your bodies* are members of Christ himself?" (1 Cor 6:15).

Actually, our response to God's mercy in salvation should be the presentation of our bodies to God for his use. It is not enough to give him our hearts, our heads, our prayers, or our souls. He wants our bodies. "In view of God's mercy . . . *offer your bodies* . . . this is your spiritual act of worship" (Rom 12:1). Using our bodies to serve and worship God is a spiritual act. God himself has taken up residence in our bodies: "Your *body* is a temple of the Holy Spirit . . . you were bought at a price. Therefore honor God *with your body*" (1 Cor 6:19–20). What better way to honor God with our bodies than to use them in his worship?

Any Evangelical dichotomy between spiritual worship and use of our bodies in that worship is hard to reconcile with these verses. In the light of all this, is it any wonder that Catholics believe God wants us to involve our bodies in his worship?

There is also good historical precedent for an actively physical worship. A twist of history convinced me that this emphasis on the physical can actually be traced to the apostles themselves.

Most Evangelicals remember how Philip met an Ethiopian eunuch on the road to Gaza. The eunuch believed and was baptized, and the two went their separate ways (Acts 8:26–39). The eunuch went to what is now Sudan. Historically reliable tradition tells us that there was only one other early missionary contact with this part of Africa—the apostle Matthew went there as a missionary.

Because of the difficulty of traveling in that part of the world, there was no more outside Christian contact for about three hundred years. As Warren H. Carroll recounts in his history, when Christian missionaries again made the trip, they found that much of Christianity had been lost. One thing that struck the missionaries, however, was that the Africans knew how to make the sign of the cross. Given their isolation, there are only two reasonable explanations: either, during the short time they interacted, Philip taught the eunuch to cross himself and the eunuch then passed the practice on; or Matthew himself taught the Africans directly. Either way, the practice of making the sign of the cross can be traced directly back to the apostles themselves.

Of course, it might be said that the Bible never teaches us to make the sign of the cross. True. The practice actually appears to predate the writing of the New Testament. It was never written about because it was never questioned. The early Christians believed in a harmony between the physical and spiritual.

Our goal in worship should not be to simplify it as much as possible. It should be to make it as rich as God desires. King David was certainly not stingy with God when he danced for him in full view of his subjects (2 Sam 6 and 1 Chron 15). Evangelicals seem to feel that less is better. This is evident not only in their use of the body but even in the calendar. All Evangelicals use the Catholic Church's calendar for some events, such as Christmas and Easter. Yet they turn around and call it ritualistic when Catholics celebrate other events, such as Pentecost or the Annunciation.

Evangelical leaders are masters of marketing. They ask themselves, "How would twentieth-century Americans like to worship?" They have made a science of answering that question well. Catholics unapologetically start at the other end of the equation. The bishops ask, "How does God desire that we worship him?" The answer may or may not fit in with individual American preferences. That is not the issue. God's opinion of our worship is of paramount importance.

The anti-physical bias of Evangelicals has other implications outside of kinds of worship. It creates fertile ground for a vague notion of an invisible church of believers, unconnected by any physical or visible unity, yet somehow one, just as God is one (Jn 17:20–21).

I understand the origin of the belief. The reformers had to explain how a person's body could be part of the body of Christ and yet not appear to be in physical communion with another person. "Do you not know that your *bodies* are members of Christ himself?" (1 Cor 6:15). For fifteen hundred years it was the understanding of all Christians that the Church was a visible entity on earth. The Church was the physical manifestation of the mystical body of Christ. This is a favorite theme of Paul. A majority of Christians still do believe this. But the reformers had to find a justification for splitting from that visible Church. They invented the notion of an invisible church. It certainly has no explicit scriptural basis.

In fact, it flies in the face of certain passages. Matthew 5:14 is a good illustration: "You are the light of the world. A city on a hill cannot be hidden." Do Evangelicals believe that their *invisible* church corresponds to a city on a hill? They themselves view the invisible church as more of an underground resistance, an invisible but influential force for good. Their church exists outside the physical realm.

There are other insurmountable problems with an invisible church. By definition, it includes only true believers, yet that directly contradicts the description of the Church that Jesus himself gives us. To qualify as Christ's Church, we must be able to find tares among the wheat (Mt 13:24–30; also Mt 13:47–52).

Given their discomfort with anything physical, is it any wonder that Evangelicals have difficulty with the most visible, non-divine person involved in the Incarnation? She anchors the person of Christ firmly in the physical realm in which we live. We shall look at Mary next.

IX

Mary

Catholic theology about Mary is so disturbing to most Evangelicals that it is difficult to explore it without emotion. Former evangelical Kimberly Hahn has said that there were three reasons she resisted Catholicism: Mary, Mary, and Mary.

My own feelings for Mary were probably very representative of those of other Evangelicals—I never thought much about her. I did not particularly love her, nor did I specifically hate her. If anything, I was a bit afraid to think too much about Mary, because of the Catholic "problem". I did not believe that Catholic doctrine concerning Mary could be found in the Bible. It was only after I appreciated the Evangelical problem with authority that I understood why Catholics are rightfully satisfied when they see that their tradition and the Bible do not contradict one another.

From my own experience, I can definitely say that Evangelicals do not talk about Mary very much. I estimate that I have listened to more than four thousand sermons by evangelicals and fundamentalists. Since most of them were well over thirty minutes long, that means over two thousand hours of listening. Included were Mother's Day sermons and Christmas sermons. There were sermons centered on the lives of Hannah, Debra, Elizabeth, Rachel, Leah, Sarah, and Eve. Not once, however, did I sit through a sermon whose central subject was Mary!

When I discussed this with an Evangelical minister, his only response was, "Well, of course, you know why that is." Could it be that Evangelicals are afraid of sounding Catholic, so they ignore a major player in the Incarnation? Why doesn't it bother Evangelicals that they are failing to fulfill the words of the Holy Spirit through Mary: "From now on all generations will call me blessed" (Lk 1:48)? Are Evangelicals basing their theology on the truth or on a fear of being labeled Catholic? All of these questions enter my mind now.

But at the beginning of my pilgrimage, one aspect of Catholic teaching on Mary kept me from investigating the Church's teaching on any subject. That was the firm insistence of the Church that Mary remained virgin her whole life and therefore had no more children after Jesus. This assertion seemed to fly in the face of the Bible verses that speak of the brothers and sisters of Jesus. When most Evangelicals refer to the virginity of Mary, they do not imply that she remained a virgin after Jesus' birth.

By reading Protestant scholars, I eventually came to the conclusion that the Catholic Church was right about Mary's perpetual virginity. And this was before I seriously considered that learning about Mary might open the door to my becoming Catholic.

We should take the language of the Bible at face value whenever possible. It struck me one day that when the Bible uses the word "brother" for a relative of Jesus, it could not possibly mean that literally. No one could have the same father as Jesus did, so the word "brother" cannot be taken at face value. All Evangelicals should agree that the closest sibling possible to Jesus would be a half-brother. This opened my mind to investigating just what the word "brother" can mean.

In English, we lack words that are necessary to other cultures. Eskimos have multiple words for snow, whereas we have only one. The different conditions of snow are very important to their daily existence. Conversely, some languages of the world lack words that English speakers think are necessary. One example is the way in which different cultures describe their relatives.

I have a friend who was born into a Hindu family in Nepal. Dan came to the United States for education after becoming an Evangelical Christian. One evening, over dinner, he was telling our family about his uncles. I was amazed at the size of his family, until I found out that the men he was describing as "uncles" included all male relatives of his parents. English speakers would call these relatives cousins, second cousins, uncles, second uncles, or in-laws. To a Nepalese, they were all "uncles". What is significant to our discussion is that Dan described them as uncles although he was speaking English! Although he is fluent in English and has even complained about losing his ability to think and speak Nepalese, he continues to use the categories of the Nepal language and culture to describe his family.

How do language and culture affect our thinking about Mary and her family? The Gospel writers reflected their culture just as Dan does his. Although Greek has a word for cousin, Aramaic, the language of the Jews, does not. Cousins were referred to with the same words used for brothers and sisters. This is even evident in the Old Testament: "So Abram said to Lot . . . 'we are brothers' " (Gen 13:8). Abraham and Lot were not brothers, but there was no Hebrew word for their relationship. Cousins, nephews, and similar male relatives were called "brother". In other words, any verses that refer to the "brothers" of Jesus are irrelevant to the question of whether Jesus actually had siblings (or half-siblings). They could easily be cousins, just as the Church has held from the very beginning.

Nor does it prove anything that Jesus is described as Mary's "firstborn" in Luke 2:7. Firstborn was a technical term, as in firstborn lamb, which did not necessarily imply a second-born. Although this usage sounds strange in English, there are other examples of a single offspring being called "firstborn".

Some Evangelicals point to the use of "until" in Matthew 1:25: "But he [Joseph] had no union with her [Mary] until she gave birth to a son." They claim that, logically, this surely means there were relations after Jesus was born. Once again, we must not make the verse imply what it never meant to say. The focus of the verse is the fact that Jesus was not, nor could he possibly have been, the son of Joseph.

Psalm 110 is a messianic psalm, in which God tells the Messiah to sit at his side while he subjugates his enemies: "Sit at my right hand until I make your enemies a footstool for your feet" (Ps 110:1). Here the word "until" is used without an implication that Jesus would not be welcome at the right hand of the Father after his enemies were subjugated. Michal, King David's wife, is described as having "no children until the day of her death" (2 Sam 6:23). The "until" certainly does not mean she gave birth after her death. The biblical use of "until", therefore, does not support a claim that Mary ever had relations with Joseph.

There is simply no Bible passage that refutes Mary's perpetual virginity. I took it as a very important confirmation that, without exception, all the early creeds of the Church described Mary as "ever-virgin". The early Church entertained no confusion on this issue.

Mary, the wife of Clopas, is the key to the puzzle (Jn

19:25). She seems to have been Mary's sister-in-law. The two families may even have shared a home together, a common arrangement in Israel at that time. Scripture specifically tells us that she is the mother of James and his siblings (Mt 27:56; Mk 15:40, 16:1; Lk 24:10). If Mary, wife of Clopas, was the mother of James, then obviously Mary, wife of Joseph, was not.

As I studied the issue of Mary's virginity, I realized that there was no proof either way in Scripture. So why not accept that Jesus was the only child of Mary, just as the Church has always maintained? Even the major Protestant reformers accepted Mary's perpetual virginity.

On reflection, Mary's perpetual virginity makes the most sense. Even without a vow of celibacy, can anyone doubt that Joseph would have refrained from marital relations with the woman who bore the very Son of God? Think about that question for a moment. Although Catholics have pondered that question for generations, it is a rare Evangelical who has had it cross his mind. It is an implication of the Incarnation that Evangelicals would rather ignore.

Why was this fact about Mary never included in Scripture? Probably because it was commonly known. She was still alive when the Bible was being written. It was easy to determine the facts. Just ask her or the many people who knew her. Tradition tells us she was under the care of John until she died (the Dormition) in Jerusalem around A.D. 49.

Did other people of that time make vows of virginity and celibacy? Yes, recent discoveries (such as at Qumran) leave no doubt that it was a known practice, though uncommon. But surely Evangelicals and Catholics would agree that Mary and Joseph were an uncommon couple. What common couple would have been entrusted with the early education of God incarnate?

John is quite clear, in Revelation 14:4, that virginity is a superior way to follow God: "They kept themselves pure." Paul certainly accepts marriage relations as holy and undefiled. Yet he teaches that abstinence is better still: "I would like you to be free from concern . . . a married man is concerned about the affairs of this world . . . his interests are divided. . . . I am saying this for your own good . . . that you may live in . . . undivided devotion to the Lord" (1 Cor 7:32–35).

I have observed the mental gymnastics of Evangelicals while trying to explain the identity of the virgin referred to in 1 Corinthians 7:32–38. The most straightforward explanation is that she is the virgin wife (or betrothed) of a celibate missionary. They have taken the course of chastity within marriage (or betrothal, which was more of a commitment than an engagement is today) in order to further God's kingdom, just as Mary and Joseph did. The practice of remaining celibate within marriage (or betrothal) seems to have become somewhat common in the early Church. It became even more common during the Middle Ages.

There was a period of time while I was studying at Trinity when my roommate's girlfriend would not even speak to me. James and I had been discussing Scripture and its requirements for a godly life. We both wanted to experience God's best. We tentatively came to the conclusion that Scripture held up the celibate-virgin lifestyle as the best way to serve God. We finally changed our minds when we could find no support for the concept anywhere in Evangelicalism. The most common explanation for the pertinent passages was that they did not apply to the twentieth-century church. But, in the meantime, my roommate's girlfriend was very unhappy with me. She mistakenly assumed that I was responsible for the conclusions James and I had reached together.

Catholics sometimes have difficulty understanding why the concept of celibacy is such a major issue with Evangelicals. After all, it is quite clear in the Bible. Actually, I believe it often has very little to do with the scriptural data and much more to do with the practical implications of the elevation of celibacy and virginity as a way to please God.

We must remember that Evangelicals are led by leaders who are married. It was common knowledge when I was in seminary that it can be very difficult to place a single man in a church as pastor. This is in spite of the fact that the ministry is extremely hard on a minister's family. (A recent survey concluded that about one-half of all Protestant ministers would not enter the ministry if they had it to do all over again. The primary reason was the tremendous stress on the family.) Many seminarians enter school single but are married by the time placements are made.

The leadership of Evangelicalism is not in a position even to consider whether it is as focused on Christ's mission as it should be. Paul's exhortations can be explained away. Mary's example can be denied. The historical precedent of the early Church can be ignored. But the leadership of Evangelicalism must preserve its reputation for total devotion, in spite of the distractions of marriage. I am not criticizing these men. Given the organizational structure of the churches in which they must operate, they have an almost unbelievable job. Burn-out is not uncommon, and it is totally understandable. The last thing they need is someone questioning their commitment.

Given her part in the Incarnation, it makes perfect sense that Mary would become a central resource and role model for the early Church. Who else could have told Luke of the Annunciation, the trip to Elizabeth, or the Virgin Birth? It was only natural for early Christians to visit Mary and to ask her to pray for them. Evangelicals certainly ask each other to pray for their urgent requests today. And after Mary died, why not continue to ask her to pray for certain needs and requests?

Some Evangelicals would respond, "Don't talk to a dead person, because that is 'necromancy'!" But they are very confused. Webster's says that necromancy is "the act or practice of trying to foretell the future or the unknown by alleged communication with the dead". This is what King Saul did when he visited the Witch of Endor (1 Sam 28). He wanted the dead prophet Samuel to act as a fortuneteller for him.

I know of no Catholic who asks Mary or a saint for prayers in the hope of seeing the future. Just as I know of no Evangelical who asks his Bible study group for prayers in the hope that they will forecast the future.

Catholics firmly believe that so-called "dead" Christians are very much alive in Christ. Membership in the Church is not terminated at death. That is why the prayers of saints should still be asked for, just as we ask for the prayers of living Christians. That is the reason Catholics petition Mary and other Christians who have died. They are asking these saints to pray to God for them. If we all agree that they are alive in Christ (few Evangelicals accept the doctrine of soul sleep), then they can pray to God for us full time. There is no doubt their prayers will be effective: "Pray for each other. . . . The prayer of a righteous man is powerful and effective" (James 5:16; see Rev 8:3–4).

Some Evangelicals claim that they have no need of anyone other than God. If they are right, then they must be stronger than Jesus himself. Even he availed himself of the services of both saints and angels (Mt 4:11, Lk 22:43, Mk 9:2).

It is in this light that we should approach the Rosary. When Catholics "pray the Rosary", they ask nothing of Mary that she cannot fulfill. They are asking Mary for her prayers to God on their behalf. When the practice of the Rosary is examined from a strictly Evangelical viewpoint, it is seen to be not so much a prayer as a time of meditation on the Incarnation. This is another subject on which we have miscommunication. Catholics call the Rosary "prayer" because their definition of prayer tends to be broader than that of the typical Evangelical. Catholics use prayer both for conversation with God (as do Evangelicals) and also in the older sense of a serious petition—"any earnest request or entreaty" (*Webster's New World Dictionary*).

It was not until after I espoused Catholicism that I began to grasp the purpose of the Rosary. My emotions could not handle the idea of talking to someone who had died. Colleen did not have this problem. Her father died when she was a teenager. Since then, she has often had the firm assurance that he still cared about her life and could hear her.

Catholics had tried to explain the Rosary to me. A good friend had tried to get me to understand it six years before I reconciled to Catholicism. The idea was just not appealing to me—it seemed like idolatry or superstition. My misconceptions are relatively common. I have yet to discuss the Rosary with an Evangelical who understands it. Yet we all felt confident in condemning the practice.

One issue most Evangelicals have to deal with is the beads. Why have them? I had the same question. Since I began using them, however, I have found them invaluable. I sometimes have problems concentrating my mind on prayer and meditation for a substantial length of time. The movement of my fingers over the beads keeps my mind engaged. The different shapes and sizes of the beads enable me to concentrate on prayer, because my fingers are assisting my mind. In addition to using my fingers, I use my voice and my ears to keep my mind concentrated. Unless someone has a firmly entrenched dislike of anything physical in worship, I believe he will find the rosary beads a definite aid to serious prayer and meditation. Remember, we are not bodiless angels.

The Rosary consists of a series of prayers, although not all of them would be considered prayers by Evangelicals. The first step is the recital of the Apostles' Creed. I included the text of this in the first section, so I will not include it here. It is one of the oldest formulations of the Christian faith in existence. Evangelicals accept it as authentic and orthodox, although they do not accept it as authoritative. Reciting it reminds Catholics of the basics of the Christian faith, and it brings glory to God when they proclaim their belief in all of it.

The second step is the Lord's Prayer (the Our Father). Since most Christians are familiar with the Lord's Prayer, it does not need to be included here (see Mt 6:9–13). Praying the words of Jesus puts Catholics into the mindset that Jesus intended for prayer.

I should probably mention that when I first heard Catholics recite the Lord's Prayer, I was shocked that they left out the last phrase: "For thine is the kingdom, and the power, and the glory forever. Amen." They ended on the word "evil". On further investigation I found that modern New Testament scholars now believe that the most reliable ancient manuscripts substantiate the Catholic version of this prayer. Evangelical versions include later interpolations (from 1 Chron 29:11) that Jesus did not originally teach his disciples. Yet for generations Protestants trusted their Bibles (translated from unreliable manuscripts) instead of accepting the reliable tradition of the Church. This is one more example of how the bishops preserved the truth even better than the written word could.

A little later, the Glory Be is prayed. It proclaims: "Glory be to the Father and to the Son and to the Holy Spirit. As it was in the beginning, is now, and ever shall be, world without end. Amen." Certainly this is a prayer based on biblical concepts.

For most of the Rosary the participant will alternate Hail Marys with the Lord's Prayer and the Glory Be. Generally, ten Hail Marys will be said between each Lord's Prayer and Glory Be.

Although this involves repetition, that certainly should not cause Evangelicals to stumble. We all repeat prayers. Sometimes our repetitions are separated by seconds, sometimes by hours, sometimes by days. But we don't use completely new phrases and thoughts every time we pray. In fact, Jesus praised the widow for dogged repetition in her prayer requests (Lk 18:1–8). In heaven, God is continually praised day and night with the repetition of the words "Holy, holy, holy is the Lord God Almighty, who was, and is, and is to come" (Rev 4:8). What Jesus roundly condemned was mindless, unfocused repetition of prayers (Mt 6:7). So do Catholic books about the Rosary. Our minds and souls must remain engaged for prayer to be effective.

The use of a prepared prayer of this sort is unfamiliar to some Evangelicals. Once again, we must remember that this practice has solid biblical precedent. The Psalms are a compilation of prepared prayers. Jesus himself often prayed them. Paul tells us to use the Psalms as well (Eph 5:19, Col 3:16). Even Evangelicals pray prepared texts when singing certain hymns. "Great Is Thy Faithfulness" is one example of a memorized prayer set to music.

What is the Hail Mary? Primarily, it is the quoting of Scripture. Once I examined the actual words, I was left with the question, "Why did I mindlessly resist this prayer so long?" This is how the prayer goes:

"Hail Mary, full of grace. The Lord is with you." This is

taken directly from Luke 1:28. It is the greeting of the angel Gabriel to Mary.

"Blessed are you among women." This is from Luke 1:42. It is the greeting to Mary by Elizabeth, who was filled with the Holy Spirit at the time.

"And blessed is the fruit of your womb, Jesus." This is a minor modification of Luke 1:42. What Evangelical would have a problem with this statement, even if it weren't almost verbatim from the Bible?

"Holy Mary, Mother of God." This statement is more of a problem for Evangelicals. They do not want to call Mary "the Mother of God". Some Evangelicals think that this statement implies that Mary was the Mother of God the Father and God the Holy Spirit. But in using this title for Mary, Catholics are affirming that she is the Mother of Jesus, and Jesus is God. That is the unmistakable meaning of Elizabeth in Luke 1:43: "But why am I so favored, that the mother of my Lord should come to me?"

Evangelicals try to avoid giving Mary the title of Mother of God, while at the same time they affirm that Jesus was God from his conception. They attempt to say that Mary was the mother only of the human nature of Jesus. But my mother was not the mother of my human nature. She was the mother of me, the person. In avoiding the use of this title for Mary, Evangelicals have inadvertently opened the door to those who question the union of the divine and the human natures in the God-man. It should not surprise anyone that only two out of five self-proclaimed evangelicals (43 percent) will agree that Jesus was both fully man and fully God (*Christianity Today*, April 18 and May 2, 1980). That is less than half!

The Evangelical solution just does not hold water, however. Either Jesus was divine from the beginning, and Mary was his mother, or somehow his divinity was separated from that child carried in the womb. (Nowhere is this Evangelical ambivalence about the Incarnation more evident than in the Evangelical notions of Christmas. Evangelicals celebrate "the miracle of Christmas". But from a strictly biblical perspective, the miracle occurred at the conception of Jesus by the Holy Spirit. The birth was a natural result of that earlier miracle, nine months before. The Annunciation is the proper time to celebrate "the miracle of Christmas".) Much better simply to agree with Elizabeth when she spoke while filled with the Holy Spirit. Mary is the mother of the child Jesus, who is our Lord and our God (Jn 20:28).

"Pray for us sinners, now and at the hour of our death." This is the end of the Hail Mary and is the only request made of Mary in the Rosary. Catholics are requesting her prayers, just as Evangelicals request the prayers of others in a Bible study group. Before starting the Rosary, it is customary to tell Mary what specific request is in one's heart. This is called an "intention". Catholics are sure that Mary is with God, she can hear us, and she cares (Heb 12:1).

But Evangelicals miss something important. During the entire Rosary, Catholics meditate on the mysteries of the Incarnation. It is customary to meditate on three sets of events in the life of Christ, using one set on various days of the week. Some pray all three sets each day. The joyful mysteries encompass the coming of Christ into the world. The sorrowful mysteries recap the events surrounding the crucifixion. The glorious mysteries cover the Resurrection and the events that followed it.

For example, the five sorrowful mysteries are the agony in the garden of Gethsemane, the scourging, the crowning with thorns, the carrying of the cross, and the crucifixion. It is a rare Evangelical who would not benefit from thinking more on these events. Many practicing Catholics spend about fifteen minutes every day on one of these sets of mysteries.

One of the mysteries in the life of Mary that bothers Evangelicals is her Assumption. It is the Catholic belief that Mary was bodily assumed into heaven at the point of her death (either right before or right after). When I looked objectively at the dogma, it was a little difficult to understand the vociferousness with which Evangelicals attack it. Mary certainly was not the first person to be taken physically up to heaven at or before death. Both Enoch and Elijah (and some say Moses) experienced this before they died (Gen 5:24; Heb 11:5; 2 Kings 2:10–12). Could it be a problem to some Evangelicals that the others are men and Mary is a woman?

Perhaps this belief is attacked because it is not contained in the Bible. But, as we have already shown, that does not mean that a teaching is not true. The teaching of the Assumption can be found in writing at least fourteen hundred years ago. The bishops of the Church tell us that it is a part of the original deposit of truth verbally handed down from the apostles. It was widely debated during the Middle Ages. Both Catholic and Orthodox Churches accept it as true, although it was not formally defined by the Church until 1950. The Pope built his defining document on the universal teaching of the second-century Fathers of the Church. This teaching linked Mary and Eve to the redemption and the Fall.

When I investigated the Assumption for my own knowledge, it struck me as very significant that no city or church of the ancient world has ever claimed to be the permanent burial place of Mary. Nor has anyone claimed to have the bones of Mary, as various groups have done with other saints (such as John the Baptist). This is almost inconceivable, when one considers the reverence in which the early heroes of the

faith were held. After their death, martyrs' bones were immediately collected and preserved by the early Christians. Mary
was a hero of the first order. Yet no one ever claimed to have
her bones. The most reasonable explanation for this is that it
was common knowledge that Mary's body had been taken up
into heaven.

Evangelicals rightly answer the sceptics of the Resurrection by asking them to produce the body of Jesus. Catholics
can ask the same of Evangelical sceptics concerning Mary's
Assumption—find us the body.

The Assumption of Mary does not seem unusual at all if
one accepts the Immaculate Conception. This is the teaching
that Mary was preserved from inheriting the effects of original sin. Some Evangelicals think this teaching means that
Mary was born of a virgin, just as Jesus was. This is just one
more example of the misunderstandings Evangelicals may
have concerning Catholic dogma.

Actually, the Immaculate Conception seems to be an outrageous doctrine to Evangelicals. If one accepts the Evangelical teaching on the effects of Adam's original sin, then one
would have to agree that the Immaculate Conception is implausible. Both Evangelicals and Catholics teach that we inherit the effects of original sin because Adam disobeyed in
the Garden of Eden. But they disagree about what the effects
of original sin are.

Evangelicals teach that at creation God made man fully
human. As a part of his human nature, he had fellowship with
God. When Adam sinned, he lost that fellowship and became
less than fully human. The original sin resulted in what Evangelicals call "total depravity". This means that there is absolutely nothing good in any man or in the actions of any man.
Some Evangelicals would go so far as to say that even man's
rational abilities are now defective. Man's tendency toward

evil is insurmountable. At the Fall, mankind lost traits and abilities that were innately part of being fully human.

By the Evangelicals' own admission, this does not fit reality as we experience it: "That sin renders the sinner totally depraved cannot be read from human experience" (*Zondervan's Pictorial Encyclopedia*). Because this scenario does not ring true, the reformers invented a doctrine called "common grace". Since that is not germane to our discussion of Mary, we will leave it at that.

Catholics have always taught that man was created fully human. But God endowed man with extra gifts (grace) that enabled him to have perfect fellowship with God and to have total control over his physical body. This is called the state of "original justice". These gifts were something above and beyond being fully human. No one could rightfully demand that these extra gifts be an integral part of his own personal human experience. They were extras.

The result of original sin was the loss of these extra gifts that were originally given to Adam. This meant that man, after the Fall of Adam, was unable to please God or to have fellowship with him. He also had an undeniable inclination to do wrong rather than right (concupiscence). He lost the total control over his body. Yet the Fall did *not* make him less than the fully human creature he was at his creation.

A mathematical comparison might shed some light on the issue. Evangelicals teach that Adam was created at zero, and, when he fell into original sin, he fell to negative one. Catholics teach that man was created at zero and immediately given extra gifts that brought him to positive one. When Adam fell, mankind descended to zero but still was fully human.

So we can see that, from the Evangelical perspective, an Immaculate Conception would have been much more of a phenomenal miracle than it would be from the Catholic viewpoint. Assuming an Evangelical definition, the Immaculate Conception would entail God's reaching down and making Mary almost God-like, in contrast to the rest of humanity.

But what Catholics mean by the Immaculate Conception is that Mary was given the gift of fellowship with God from the very beginning of her life in the womb. She experienced God's grace her whole life. Most Catholics have this communion with God restored at infant baptism. Because of Mary's close fellowship with God, he enabled her to live her entire life without sinning. This does not mean Mary did not need a Savior. Like all of humanity, both before and after the Cross, she was redeemed by the precious Blood of her Son.

This is the teaching of the Church. It is not nearly so dramatic as Evangelicals tend to think. Part of the misunderstanding is because we use the same words to mean different things.

Is there any Scripture that directly teaches the Immaculate Conception? No. But there are two Scripture passages that lend themselves to this understanding of Mary's life. (Remember that it is not necessary for all dogma to be contained in Scripture.)

The most important one is in Luke: "The angel went to her and said, 'Greetings, you who are highly favored! The Lord is with you'" (1:28). Jerome probably did the best job of translating this passage so many centuries ago. He translated it as "Hail, full of grace". The important point to notice is that Mary is not addressed by Gabriel as "Mary". She is addressed as "full of grace", as though that were her name. When we unpack the Greek meaning of these words, Gabriel called Mary "The One Most Full of God's Gracious Gift of His Life in All Time".

By definition, being full of God's grace means an absence of sin. If Mary was more full of God's life than anyone in history, that statement includes Eve. We all know that Eve started life without original sin. Although the passage is not explicit, it certainly makes sense that Mary also must have started life without original sin. Otherwise, Eve would have been given the name "The One Most Full of God's Gracious Gift of His Life in All Time". The original Greek also implies that this state of being full of God's grace is not limited by time. Mary always was (since her conception) and always will be (for the rest of her life) full of the grace of God. To make this possible, Mary must have lived a life without sin.

The other pertinent passage is in Genesis: "I will put enmity between you and the woman, and between your offspring and hers; he will crush your head, and you will strike his heel" (3:15). I used to teach a class on messianic prophecy. We started with this passage. The vast majority of Evangelicals see this as the first messianic prophecy of the Old Testament. Even some of the Jewish commentators before Christ interpreted it this way. If Jesus the Messiah is the offspring, then who is the woman? That it is Mary is certainly logical. That conclusion is bolstered by other references to Mary as "woman". " 'Dear woman, why do you involve me?' Jesus replied" (Jn 2:4; see also Rev 12).

If Mary is the woman, God has said that there will always be enmity between Satan and Mary. Although this statement certainly does not prove the point, we can reasonably expect that Mary would have to be preserved by God from her mortal enemy right from the beginning. If she had been born in the state of original sin, she would have been a subject of Satan's dominion, and she and Satan would not have been at enmity with one another.

In harmony with the passage starting in Revelation 11:19, the Catholic Church likens Mary to the ark of the covenant. She bore for nine months the fullness of God's presence, just as the ark had held it in the days of Moses. She was overshadowed by God, just as the ark had been (Lk 1:35; see also Ex 40:34–35). The Old Covenant ark had been kept pure at God's command. Would we expect God to do any less in the New Covenant?

There is no longer any doubt in my mind that this belief in Mary's Immaculate Conception dates from the beginning of the Church. If Adam had never sinned, God's plan included an immaculate conception for all of us. We would all have been in fellowship with God from the start. As history unfolded, there were only four people who started life without original sin: Adam, Eve, Mary, and Jesus. God's plan for Christians is for all of us to enter heaven without the effects of original sin on our souls. It no longer strikes me as odd that God preserved the Mother of his Son from intimate contact with sin.

There are four other titles for Mary that particularly annoy Evangelicals. I know they do, because they used to annoy me. I did not understand how Catholics used these titles, and so I assumed the worst. They sounded to me as if they were either worshipping Mary or putting her on a par with her Son.

The first of these is "Queen of Angels", and the second is the related title, "Queen of Heaven". Yet there is good biblical support for both of these concepts. All Christians will one day be "judges of angels". "Do you not know that we will judge angels?" (1 Cor 6:3). If we are their judges, is it so strange that the Mother of Jesus would be called their Queen? There is certainly nothing unscriptural about the concept.

"Queen of Heaven" has its foundation firmly in Scripture: "A great and wondrous sign appeared in heaven: a woman clothed with the sun, with the moon under her feet and a crown of twelve stars on her head" (Rev 12:1). Although Evangelicals may not agree that this passage speaks of Mary, they should be willing to admit that this is a possible interpretation. An important clue is to be found in the next verses. This same woman is described as being the Mother of Jesus: "She was pregnant and cried out in pain as she was about to give birth. . . . She gave birth to a son, a male child, who will rule all the nations with an iron scepter" (Rev 12:2–5). Even Evangelicals admit that the "male child" is Jesus. I thought that the Catholic interpretation of this passage was more honest with the text than the Evangelical interpretation long before I considered Catholicism as a personal alternative. Mary is the only woman who ever gave birth to Jesus. Certainly no *group* of people can lay claim to being his mother. The title "Queen of Heaven" is certainly a logical conclusion from this text. A "crown of twelve stars" has to signify something.

The third of these misunderstood titles is "Co-Redemptrix". If Mary shares in the work of our redemption, then it seemed only logical to my Evangelical mind that this puts her on an equal footing with Christ. But I had not bothered to find out what Catholics themselves mean by this title. I discovered that even I serve as a "co-redeemer" with Christ whenever I help in the spiritual pilgrimage of another person. Colleen and I are the "co-redeemers" of each of our children. We have endeavored to bring them to Christ. If we have succeeded in any small way, it is because Christ has been laboring together with us. His is the essential part, but it is still true that we participated in their redemption: "Whoever turns a sinner from the error of his way will save him" (James 5:20). "Be merciful to those who doubt . . . and save them" (Jude 22; see also 1 Tim 4:16).

That makes us "co-redeemers" in the same sense though to a lesser degree than Mary. If for no other reason, Mary is involved in our redemption because she allowed God to use her womb to enter the physical arena. She has cooperated in bringing salvation to all of us.

It is in very much the same sense that Catholics use the final title that bothered me—"Mediatrix of all grace". Let us start at the beginning. Evangelicals can agree that Christ is the source of all of God's grace. Evangelicals also agree that the Son's mission was possible only after he was incarnated. What they sometimes fail to remember is that the Incarnation was possible only when Mary agreed to it. It is inconceivable that God the Holy Spirit would force himself on Mary to enable God the Son to become human. Mary did say Yes to Gabriel, and it was then that the Incarnation became a reality. Of course, God knew she would say Yes, but that is beside the point. In giving birth to Christ, Mary mediated God's graces (Christ) to all of humanity. From a strictly historical basis, it is hard to argue that Mary was not the Mediatrix of all God's grace.

The Catholic Church teaches, however, that God has continued this arrangement for purposes of his own. Mary still mediates the grace of Christ to his Church. This is at least partially rooted in the concept of Mary's being the new Eve. Just as Christ's obedience is in contrast to Adam's disobedience, so Mary's mediating of God's grace (Christ) to us is in contrast to Eve's mediating of Satan's temptation to Adam. Eve made sin possible through her mediation. Mary made redemption possible through her mediation. This was a popular theme of virtually all of the Fathers of the Church in the second century.

The Church is very clear that Mary's role depends on the basis of Christ and his position: "This title is so understood that it neither takes away anything from nor adds anything to the dignity and efficacy of Christ the one Mediator. Mary's role of mediatrix thus *depends on Christ's* mediatorship" (Our Sunday Visitor's *Catholic Encyclopedia*).

Christ is the "one mediator between God and man" (1 Tim 2:5). Yet, Christ has chosen to share that function with others. In verses one and two of this same chapter (1 Tim 2), Paul exhorts all Christians to be mediators. The word he uses is "intercession". Mary mediates for us to a unique degree, but because of God's command we are all mediators of God's grace to the world.

There are those who would question Christ's decision to share his responsibilities with Mary. I can say only that it makes every bit as much sense as allowing men to be the spreaders of Christ's gospel. God or his angels could evangelize the world without us. Our job is not to question why (with God); ours is only to do. "Mary's function . . . in no way obscures or diminishes this unique mediation of Christ, but rather shows its power. . . . [It] flows forth from the superabundance of the merits of Christ, rests on his mediation, depends entirely on it, and draws all its power from it. No creature [Mary] could ever be counted along with the Incarnate Word and Redeemer" (CCC 970).

Actually, Mary's whole role in life is to further the exaltation of her Son and her Savior. Catholics point to Mary at the wedding feast, where Jesus changed the water into wine. She said, "Do whatever he tells you" (Jn 2:5). She is always pointing Christians to Jesus; she is always telling us to obey him.

The Church's teaching on Mary is not a central dogma of Catholicism in the same way that her teaching on Jesus and his atonement is. After we had been attending Catholic Mass for several months, Colleen stopped me on the way out. She commented that in all that time we had never said a prayer to Mary and had hardly ever heard her name mentioned in the Mass, outside of the Nicene Creed. I was surprised also. I guess I had been a little afraid of Mary. I did not want her to supplant Jesus somehow. No fear. Our worship of Jesus is not a zero sum game. If we honor his Mother as Scripture says we should, we are not detracting from the rightful worship of our Savior.

X

Premillennialism and Eschatology

When Colleen and I decided that we would become Catholics, we discussed those issues that would be the hardest for certain friends to handle. For many, we knew it would be Mary. For others, it might be the pope. Others would be bothered by the thought of our submission to Catholic morals. She was surprised that I insisted that our departure from premillennialism would be the major stumbling block for certain clergy we knew. She was even more amazed when it turned out that I was correct.

Premillennialism is a specific opinion about how God will lower the curtain on world history. It is one view of eschatology, which is the study of the prophecies of the "end times".

Colleen recites a favorite poem from her childhood to our children.

> *There was a little girl*
> *who had a little curl,*
> *right in the middle of her forehead.*
> *When she was good,*
> *she was very, very good,*
> *but when she was bad,*
> *she was horrid.*

The two opposite behaviors of this little girl remind me of the two extremes within Evangelicalism concerning the study of prophecy yet to be fulfilled—eschatology. There is the group in which I grew up, which attended prophecy conferences, heard sermons about the end times, and read books about how the rapture would affect the world. We knew how the tribulation would relate to the rapture and the Second Coming and all the verses to support our beliefs. Many "free" Evangelicals fit into this category. They are predominantly premillennial. Premillennialism is so important to some of them that they refuse fellowship to evangelicals who hold a different eschatological view, such as Presbyterians, Reformed, and Methodists.

My wife grew up in the other group. While they may or may not be premillennial, their interests in eschatology have as little in common with the first group as the little girl's moods had in common with each other. Their theological study does not emphasize the study of future events. They believe in the Second Coming but affirm that no one can know the time or the hour. Most of the evangelicals who feel this way attend "mainline" churches. Most Catholics have an attitude similar to these mainline evangelicals.

This section might be a puzzle to anyone, Catholic or evangelical, who is not interested in eschatology. For these people, the following discussion will seem too labored. For the first group, however, it will be much too cursory. I readily grant that there is much more I could discuss that I have eliminated, due to its complexity.

The discussion can get confusing, for it centers on a disagreement about when Christ's Second Coming will occur in relation to his earthly one-thousand-year reign. This reign of Christ is called the millennium, or Kingdom. There are three alternatives: premillennial, amillennial, and postmillennial.

Postmillennialists believe that the church must usher in a time of peace and holiness for one thousand years before Christ will come again; thus his Second Coming will be "post" (after) millennial (one thousand years). There are not a great many postmillennial Evangelicals today. Because they are similar in many respects to the amillennialists, I will not discuss them further.

Catholics and most "mainline" evangelicals are amillennial, although it is an oversimplification to think that the views of these two groups are identical. Amillennialists believe that the Christian church is the millennium spoken of in the Bible. We are in the millennium now. Christ set up his Kingdom at his first coming. The thousand years may not be exactly that long, but it speaks to an extremely long time here on earth when the church will be actively advancing the rule of Christ's Kingdom. Christ could return at any time to end the millennium. That will end history, and eternity will begin.

Most "free" Evangelicals are premillennial, especially at the lay level. Premillennialists believe that Christ's Second Coming will occur immediately prior to the thousand years of peace and holiness; thus his coming will be "pre" (before) millennial (one thousand years). During these end times, the Jewish people will once again become the primary focus of God, just as they were before the Incarnation. The period of time between the Incarnation and the millennium (and tribulation) is called the "church age". After the millennium, God will end history, and eternity will begin. By this view, we could not possibly be less than one thousand years from the end of history.

Which of these three theological systems one chooses makes a tremendous difference in how one interprets the Bible. To be fair, I need to point out that there are divergences of opinion within premillennialism, especially with regard to the timing of the rapture. I am sorry that I must gloss over some of the finer points of controversy within premillennialism, such as pretribulationalism, posttribulationalism, and midtribulationalism. In focusing on the millenial differences, I will largely ignore any discussion of the tribulation and rapture.

This diversity of belief within even so small a segment of Christianity as premillennialism illustrates one of the frustrating aspects of Protestantism in general. No one agrees with anyone else, because there is no final authority. This has led to the formation of literally hundreds of denominations, with more being added continually, as Protestantism "multiplies by division".

To simplify matters, I will deal with all premillennialist thought as though it were dispensational, for two reasons. As my former professor Dr. David Wells has pointed out in *The Search for Salvation*, dispensationalists are really the only consistent premillennialists. But more to our point, they are also the most popular eschatological movement at the lay level in American Evangelicalism. (Premillennialism is almost exclusively an American phenomenon.)

There are several reasons for this. The *Scofield Reference Bible* has been tremendously influential in promulgating premillennialism within American Evangelicalism. As that reference Bible has aged, it has been replaced by newer Bibles, such as the *Ryrie Study Bible*. All of these have notes that accompany the text of Scripture so that the average reader can "understand" the Bible better—always from a premillennial perspective. Because Evangelicals do study the Bible on their own, they have been influenced immensely by these works.

The Late Great Planet Earth is one of the all-time best sellers in American Christian literature. This book is a fictional account of how the world will react to the rapture—Christ taking the church to heaven—and great tribulation—the seven years of trial before the millennium—occurring just before the Second Coming of Jesus Christ, which will begin the thousand-year program of God for Jewish Israel. It is written from a dispensational, premillennial viewpoint, and as such it has had tremendous influence on how the average layman in America views eschatology. Laymen in Evangelical churches buy into this book's presuppositions without ever examining them.

There are two defining doctrines underlying premillennialism. The first one is the more important. Without it, premillennialism collapses. If premillennialists are wrong on this, then the system cannot be justified. The first defining doctrine is that the New Testament church is *not the fulfillment* in faith of Old Testament Israel. They believe that Old Testament Israel will be brought back into the central place of God's plan after the church has been raptured from the earth just prior to the millennium. This is still in the future. The Christian church of the present age is *not* the culmination of God's plan for mankind. It is a parenthetical period inserted into God's major focus in history: the people of Israel (ethnic Jews, as distinct from Christians). Jewish Israel and the Christian church are set against each other, and Jewish Israel is given the place of predominance.

The amillennialists believe otherwise: Jewish Israel was the forerunner for the church. The church *takes the place* of Jewish Israel in the New Covenant, and that place for the church is permanent. God will never set aside the church to resume a program with Jewish Israel. The faithful of both Covenants are included in "the Israel of God", since the New Testament does refer to the church as "Israel" (Gal 6:16, Eph 2:12, Rom 9:6).

The second defining doctrine of premillennialism depends upon the first. Premillennialists believe that the millennium is a *literal kingdom* that will last for *precisely one thousand years*. The whole world will be ruled from one capital, Jerusalem. They know the millennium has not started yet because the church is still on the earth

This is the theology in which I was raised. I studied at TEDS without ever having serious doubts about its conclusions. Its approach to the interpretation of the Bible is very literal. One of the first questions premillennialists ask an amillennialist is, "How could you reject the Bible's prediction of a literal one-thousand-year reign here on earth? Don't you believe the Bible means what it says?"

One can enter virtually any evangelical denomination as a premillennialist. But one cannot become a Catholic and remain premillennialist. Premillennialist conclusions directly contradict the teaching Magisterium of the Church. This is one of the two reasons that I never even considered Catholicism as an alternative for many years. I was sure of premillennialism. (When I was in school a person could not be on faculty at TEDS, Wheaton College, Dallas Theological Seminary, Moody Bible Institute, or a multitude of other schools unless he or she was premillennial.)

What changed my mind? The deciding factor was discovering the problems in premillennialism. Some of them are absolutely impossible to solve. Both of the defining doctrines of premillennialism can be seriously challenged from Scripture. The case for premillennialism was not the tight, open-and-shut case I had always believed it to be. If the first defining doctrine falls, particularly, this causes premillennialism to collapse. I did not learn this in seminary. I learned it from my own study of Scripture as an adult.

Most premillennialists do not know the weaknesses of

their own eschatology. Nor do they seem to be aware of the fact that it was not until the mid-nineteenth century that their theology was first clearly formulated. Except for a few isolated people, no appreciable segment of the Church accepted premillennialism for over eighteen centuries. Even now it is almost exclusively an American Evangelical phenomenon.

I started to question the second defining doctrine of premillennialism first. I came to see that it was very probable that the Bible did not mean to convey the idea of a literal one thousand years. It was not important whether I myself believed in a literal one-thousand-year millennium. The important question was whether *John* believed in it literally when he wrote Revelation. If he did not mean literally one thousand years, what right did I have to impose my presuppositions on his text? Based on my personal study of the books of Jeremiah, Daniel, and Revelation, I came to the conclusion that John probably did not mean a literal one thousand years.

Daniel contains two of the only clear, specific prophecies about time in the Bible that we can independently and accurately verify to determine whether they literally occurred. In Daniel 8:14, a period of "twenty-three hundred days" is foretold. Yet no scholars pretend that history fulfills this prophecy in exactly twenty-three hundred days. We can come close to that amount of time, but not right on the money.

The problem pops up again when Jeremiah and Daniel discuss the prediction of a seventy-year captivity of the Jews; in Jeremiah 29:10 and Daniel 9:2, "the desolation of Jerusalem would last seventy years." I discovered that even staunchly literal premillennialists, such as Dr. John F. Walvoord (*Daniel, the Key to Prophetic Revelation*), admit that those seventy years were not literally seventy years. The closest anyone seems able to get is sixty-seven years or seventy-one years.

Since God, obviously, knew the captivity would last sixty-seven or seventy-one years, instead of seventy, why the "mistake"? After all, a miss is as good as a mile if we are speaking of literal time periods. The explanation is really rather simple. It stems from a different perception of the purpose of numbers in different cultures.

An analogy is the way different cultures consider time. Americans are very literal and exacting in their use of time. "Seven o'clock" does not mean "quarter past seven o'clock" —just ask any American employer. It means "seven o'clock", or maybe even "five minutes before seven o'clock". Other cultures think differently. For them, "seven o'clock" could mean "any time between seven o'clock and eight o'clock".

What is the purpose of numbers in the Bible? Biblical numbers have an interpretation that is more important than their literal meaning. The seventy in Daniel is the result of multiplying ten and seven. These are both symbolic numbers that signify perfection and completion. The captivity of Daniel and his fellow Jews was not exactly seventy years, but it certainly was "perfectly complete". That fact was more important in the biblical prophecy than the exact number of years. Symbolism took precedence over literalism.

The twenty-three hundred days in Daniel 8:14 are primarily symbolic. That number of days is approximately six years and four months. Seven years would be a prophetically ideal time of judgment. So twenty-three hundred days symbolize a shortened period of divine judgment, indicative of God's mercy.

The lights lit up in my head when I saw that the same could hold true for the millennium in Revelation. One principle of Bible interpretation is to use the Bible to understand the Bible. One thousand is the result of multiplying ten times ten times ten: ten cubed. Ten is the number of completion or perfection. Ten years cubed symbolizes God's Kingdom lasting until it was "completely, perfectly completed". It would lack no time for its purpose. It would complete God's plan in "three dimensions". A new heaven and earth could be created, because God's program for the old one would be over, completely.

We see this use of one thousand elsewhere in Scripture. I remember as a child singing "He owns the cattle on a thousand hills, the wealth in every mine." That song is based on Psalm 50:10. No one asks, "Which thousand hills are God's?" We understand that the meaning of the number one thousand is that God's wealth is perfectly complete. He has no need for our paltry offerings.

By understanding numbers this way, we see that a literal interpretation of the twenty-three hundred days would merely inform the listeners that most people would live to see the end of the time period, about six and one-half years later. The seventy years indicates that most of those living at the beginning of the captivity would *not* live to see the end of it. Only younger children might live that long. What could one thousand years mean, literally? Even the great-grandchildren of those presently alive at the beginning of the period would not survive to see the end of the thousand years. God's millennium would be very, very long.

This verifiable Old Testament use of numbers as symbols certainly makes the Catholic, amillennial view the more probable one. It cannot be denied that it depends on a very biblical method of using numbers. But it was the evidence against the first defining doctrine of premillennialism that I found most convincing.

Premillennialists claim that Old Testament Israel is totally different from the New Testament church. The church is not a continuation of Israel, nor does it supplant Israel. In fact, in God's plan, Israel will return to center stage during the millennium (and tribulation). This is such a strongly held presupposition of premillennialists that it took the input of three separate biblical writers to convince me that it is not necessarily a biblical concept.

The first was Paul. In Romans 11:17-26, Paul uses the olive tree as an example of the plan of God throughout the ages. He wrote that the original branches (Jewish Israel) were cut off from the tree and new branches (the church) were grafted into the root (the Israel of God). I read this passage while reading through my New Testament several years before even considering Catholicism. I was not studying the passage. I was reading it simply as a part of the entire argument of Romans. I stopped and read it again, and then again.

It struck me that, if premillennialism were true, the analogy was a very poor one. Assuming premillennialism, a much better analogy would have had the first tree (Jewish Israel) go dormant, a second tree (the church) spring to life and later be removed to heaven (the rapture), and then the first tree (Jewish Israel) come back to life again (the millennium). How could Paul have had premillennial presuppositions in mind and yet use an analogy so ill-suited to them? The analogy of one tree of faith, with part of it cut off (Jewish Israel) and a new branch (the church) grafted into the original tree (the Israel of God), fit amillennial thought patterns much better. Paul spoke of only one tree, not two.

I wondered about this for about five years before the second piece of the puzzle fell into place. My presuppositions on the difference between Israel and the church did not give way easily.

When Peter preached the first Christian sermon on the day of Pentecost, he quoted from Joel 2:28-32. Virtually all Evangelicals agree that Joel was predicting the events that would occur at the start of the Kingdom (millennium). Peter applied those verses directly to the events on the day of Pentecost (Acts 2:14-41). Peter said that the Kingdom of God had started on that day. The birthday of the Church was the beginning of the Kingdom, the millennium. That would mean that the Church, the Kingdom, and the millennium were all different ways of describing the same thing. That is an amillennial mindset. That is Catholic dogma.

I knew the premillennial interpretation of this passage, but it struck me as insufficient. Its insufficiency is in fact so undeniable that one prominent Evangelical professor left a premillennial seminary in mid-career largely due to the implications of this sermon. If Peter, under the inspiration of the Holy Spirit, says that on the day of Pentecost the Kingdom has begun, then the amillennialists are right. If Peter preached that he was in the Kingdom, then obviously I am in it too. The Kingdom is synonymous with the Church age, and the leadership of the Church has taken the place of the leadership of Jewish Israel in God's plan.

For premillennialists, the only valid way around this is to try to claim that Peter was mistaken or very confused. But why would the Holy Spirit allow the birthday of the Church to be marred by such a momentous error? Why would the Church preserve Peter's sermon if she did not agree with him? The most straightforward answer is that Peter was not mistaken. Within one generation of this sermon, the sacrifices of the Jewish leaders ceased. The Church, composed of both Jew and Gentile, had become the new Israel of God, working out his plan in the millennium. Many of the structures of Israel were retained, but the leadership had been supplanted. (This, of course, is a major problem in Protestant amillennial circles. They have no continuity of leadership in the millennium.)

Still I clung half-heartedly to premillennialism. As my children well know, it takes a great deal of evidence and a long time of thinking before their father changes his mind.

The third and final straw broke the camel's back. In the Old Testament, God had his elect, the people of God. They were his chosen ones, the Jewish nation. About two hundred times in the Old Testament, a specific Hebrew word is used for them: *qahal*. When the Scriptures were translated into the Greek Septuagint, that word was translated into Greek as well. Many times the word used to translate *qahal* is *ekklesia*. Some Evangelicals will recognize the word, even though it is in Greek. In English the word means "church".

So what was the final straw? In Matthew 16:18, Jesus himself used that same word, *ekklesia*, to describe the New Testament Church he promised to build on Peter: "On this rock I will build *my* church (*ekklesia*). Since the Septuagint was the Bible of Jesus' time, we know he recognized *ekklesia* as a word associated with the Old Covenant people of God. Jesus used it only three times in the Gospels. Each time it refers to the New Testament Church. In Jesus' mind, the Old Covenant chosen people were completed and fulfilled by the New Covenant chosen people of the Church. It is unmistakable. The rest of the New Testament writers followed the lead of Jesus and used this familiar Old Testament word to describe the Christian Church as well.

There can be no reasonable explanation for Jesus' use of the word *ekklesia* other than the obvious one. Jesus used the same word for Old Testament Israel and for the New Testament Church because he knew the Church would constitute the new Israel. She would fulfill the messianic prophecies and bring the fellowship of God beyond a holy bloodline to the whole human race. She would carry on the work of God throughout the world after "his own did not receive him" (Jn 1:11). This change in God's agenda would become obvious to everyone when the temple was destroyed in A.D. 70. Jesus even predicted the destruction of the temple in the Olivet Discourse (Mt 24, Mk 13). (While at TEDS, David Palm wrote an excellent thesis [unpublished] that will help premillennialists understand better the Olivet Discourse.)

Most premillennialists seem to be unaware that Jesus used the same word for the Church as the Old Testament used for Israel. Once that is recognized, it is difficult to reconcile it with premillennialism. The only explanation I have encountered among premillennialists is shocking. Some Evangelicals have claimed that Jesus used the word *ekklesia* with Peter because he had no clear concept of the New Testament Church. Imagine! The rejection of the Messiah by Jewish Israel blindsided Jesus. In this view, Jesus himself did not understand the Old Testament messianic prophecies. And the Son of God was incarnated without a clear idea of his sacrifice and what it would accomplish. This explanation seems so preposterous, I can understand why it was eighteen centuries before anyone was bold enough to propose it.

It had taken input from the teaching of Peter, Paul, and Jesus; but I finally accepted the eschatology of the Church. Once I did, I found that many formerly problem passages yielded a treasure trove of new insights.

Because Catholic amillennialists claim that Jewish Israel, like Esau, turned its back on its birthright by rejecting Jesus, some premillennialists have accused amillennialists of being anti-Semitic. They claim that amillennialism means that the Jews inherit all the curses and the Church inherits all the blessings. They claim this eschatology gave fertile ground for the abuses of the Crusades and the Spanish Inquisition and even the atrocities of World War II in Europe.

The important question is always, "What is the scriptural position?" But in this case I decided to investigate a little history. Granting that anti-Semitism is wrong, that it did exist, and that some people within the Church had been guilty of it on various occasions, I came to the conclusion that the causal connection with Catholic, amillennial theology could not be made.

It is well known that, during the Crusades, some Jews and Jewish communities were attacked by Christian soldiers. What is not so well known is that the Catholic bishops tried to stop these attacks. They preached and pleaded. It was a sin to do what those Christian soldiers did. Sometimes the bishops were able to stop the attacks; sometimes they were not. It was not the first time or the last that the Church was ignored even though she was morally right. There was anti-Semitism, but it was not rooted in theology. The anti-Semitism was founded on historic, economic, and societal issues. Theology was used occasionally as an excuse.

The whole concept underlying the Spanish Inquisition is difficult for twentieth-century Americans to understand. Misinformation has not helped. It can be understood only in the context of a bitter eight-hundred-year war between Christians and Muslims. The temporary lulls during this long war were called the "cold war". Spain was the entire Western front in the defense of Christian Europe. Militant Islam was on the march, and many times Islam was victorious. When victorious, Muslims could be brutal with the Christians. One of the major goals of the Spanish Inquisition was to prevent non-Christians from participating in governmental office. The government of predominantly

Christian Spain was trying to assure the loyalty of its governmental workers before they might sorely need that loyalty under Muslim attack.

What is important for the present discussion, however, is often overlooked. The Spanish Inquisition did not apply to Jews. No non-Christian who publicly admitted his unbelief was supposed to be interrogated. That public act would disqualify him for government service, so that he could not harm the Christian government if it was attacked. The Inquisition's purpose was to root out religious *impostors* in powerful positions. But because Catholic leaders, like the rest of us, can sin, the purposes and methods of the Inquisition were sometimes abused and misguided. The theology of Spanish Catholicism, however, was certainly not innately anti-Semitic.

In spite of all that Catholics suffered for their faith at the hands of the Nazis, some Evangelicals have blamed the Church for Germany's "Jewish solution". Those in Europe during World War II knew better, historical revisionists notwithstanding. Thousands of priests and religious brothers were killed. Many Catholic churches, religious houses, and private homes were part of the effort to save Jews from the Nazi camps. Pope John Paul II was, as a seminarian in Poland, involved personally in the underground.

In 1945, a prominent sixty-five-year-old Jewish rabbi converted to Roman Catholicism. Because of his conversion, he called himself a "completed Jew". Talk about raising some eyebrows! He was almost immediately blackballed by the Jewish community worldwide.

Israel Zolli's story is not well known, but he was an orthodox rabbi of learning who survived World War II. As chief rabbi of Rome, he had a bird's-eye view of all that the Catholic Church did in trying to stop the Holocaust. On one occasion he even volunteered himself to the Nazi forces as a hostage, if they would release hundreds of other Italian Jews.

Is it likely that Rabbi Zolli would have joined the Roman Catholic Church if he had observed her cooperating with the Holocaust? No. In fact, he said, "I am convinced that after this war, the only means of withstanding the forces of destruction and of undertaking the reconstruction of Europe will be the acceptance of Catholicism." Not the kind of statement he would make unless he knew that the Church had done everything she could to stop the slaughter of Jews. Rabbi Zolli was offered a lifetime position at a Protestant university if he would become Protestant. But in joining the Catholic Church he joined the cause of self-sacrificing love.

Moral Issues

People have many different hobbies: golfing, swimming, running, chess. My favorite hobby is reading. I found myself somehow included on the mailing list of an excellent source for Catholic books and tapes. At first, I thought someone had played a practical joke on me. After my initial shock, I started to order books and tapes that piqued my interest.

The first Catholic writer I remember reading specifically because he was Catholic was Pope John Paul II. I quickly came to the conclusion that whatever this man was, he was not opposed to Christ and his Kingdom. Anyone who would call this Pope the anti-Christ was woefully uninformed. His thinking was thoroughly Christian, and his insights were absolutely startling.

The second author I read was Dr. Peter Kreeft. I was interested in his approach to morality. After reading one of his books, I wondered why it was Catholics who had the most profound things to say on modern ethical dilemmas. I wondered if Dr. Kreeft had ever had anyone explain Evangelical theology to him. I couldn't help thinking that someone of his caliber would respond positively to the Evangelical message. It wasn't until after I had already reconciled to the Catholic Church myself that I discovered that Peter Kreeft was also a

Catholic who had been born into evangelicalism. No doubt he already understood Evangelical theology quite well.

When it comes to moral issues, Evangelicals and Catholics build on the same foundation. We have another one of our glorious agreements. We both understand that the main purpose in our lives is to bring praise and glory to God. We are not our own; we "were bought at a price" (1 Cor 6:19). God is the foundation of our existence, and we owe him everything. This includes the living of a virtuous life. When we live virtuously, we demonstrate our love for God, and he is glorified in us. When we fail to live a virtuous life, we bring shame upon his name. On this cornerstone of morality, we could scarcely agree more completely. The very next building block is closely related to the first. We must protect the dignity of our fellow human beings because they are made in God's image. Their dignity is a reflection of God's (Lk 10:25–28).

Like many Evangelicals, I had long admired the practical stand of the Catholic Church on moral issues. The Church was one of the few institutions that stood firm against the unrelenting pressure of secular society. The Church always taught God's standards as the ideal. She taught virtue.

This is important, because the person who changes the rules for moral behavior stands under a harsher judgment than the person who knows the good but simply fails to live up to it: "Woe to those who call evil good and good evil" (Is 5:20; see also Mt 5:19). I knew enough individual Catholics to know that they were not perfect, and sometimes they were scandalously far from perfect. But Evangelicals were not perfect, either. All of us fail to live up to God's standards perfectly at one time or another. We all miss the mark. But the Catholic Church could be counted on to hold the line on moral truth in her constant, official teaching. Her modern morality was identical to her ancient morality.

As a young man, I would have said the same of Evangelicals. I no longer can. Within my lifetime, I have seen Evangelicals cave in on a multitude of moral issues. I have come to the conclusion that, at a moral level, Evangelicals are in deep trouble. Their practice is not worse than that of other groups, but their standards are being rapidly eroded. A few examples may be in order—as illustrating a change in the teaching of what is right and moral, not mere slip-ups in practical living. A change in teaching is much more ominous.

The "church growth" proponents at Fuller Seminary (a prominent evangelical school) have become famous for their insistence that Christian churches must segregate their congregations. While at TEDS, I studied under one of the leaders of this movement. They would never use the word "segregate", but for almost a generation proponents of this movement have taught that mixing cultures and races inhibits the numerical growth of churches. For example, they promote the formation of different churches for middle-class whites and for middle-class blacks. I was involved in a denomination with this philosophy. It bothered many of the laymen and pastors I knew, but the church leaders were firm in their insistence on segregation.

Like many Evangelical laymen, I had heard sermons in church advising against interethnic marriages. Some fundamentalist schools, such as Bob Jones University, even forbid interracial dating. When I found people of all races and socioeconomic backgrounds worshipping together in Catholic churches, I was ecstatic. When I looked around during one of the first Masses I attended, I saw an Oriental woman sitting in my pew, a black family in the pew ahead of me, and a Hispanic couple across the aisle. I was relieved to see that Catholic leadership taught toleration, love, and acceptance among all people.

This teaching has strong historical precedent. G. K. Chesterton noted that whenever Catholics colonized a new land, they generally intermarried with the natives after they had been Christianized. Protestants generally have not intermarried. With the common Evangelical arrangement, how are we one as the Father and Son are one? What statement do Evangelicals make concerning racism when they promote separate churches and advise against interethnic and interracial dating and marriage?

There are, of course, islands of virtue in Evangelicalism. But it is disturbing that some of the large Evangelical churches in the United States refuse to take a stand against abortion. They are afraid that the issue is too controversial. Taking a stand against it might turn off some prospective parishioners and thereby slow their church's numerical growth. Some Evangelicals do take a courageous stand against abortion, but how Christian is Evangelicalism as a whole if it fails to speak with a unified voice to the important moral issues of the day?

The Christian teaching on abortion is clear even in the first century. The *Didaché* says, "You shall not kill the human embryo by abortion." This work on Christian morality and Church polity was written about A.D. 60, before the temple in Jerusalem was destroyed and while some of the apostles were still alive.

On another moral issue, a popular Evangelical radio host has made a cassette tape series for children entering puberty. In his presentations he explains to them the changes their bodies will undergo. This is admirable, and most of the tapes are excellent. What is worrisome is his approach to masturbation. He tells his listeners that it is perfectly normal and healthy for both boys and girls to masturbate regularly. His only justification for this position seems to be that they will do it anyway, and the guilt will be damaging to them if anyone tells them it is wrong. (How tragic that this Evangelical does not understand the sacrament of Penance.) Of course, I have heard the same argument in favor of all kinds of sins. To his credit, he does admit there is Scripture that seems to teach against masturbation. The fact that *all* Christian churches of prior centuries declared that this type of impurity with oneself is wrong is never acknowledged. When his personal opinion is in opposition both to Scripture and to historical teaching, he proposes that Christians listen to him.

On another front, the retreat of Evangelicals on divorce and remarriage hardly needs to be mentioned to any observant Evangelical. I can think of several famous Evangelical preachers who once took a firm stand on this moral issue. Now that their children have grown and have encountered problems in their lives, the preachers have altered their views on the divorce and remarriage of Christians. I come from a preacher's family, and I understand what may be happening behind the scenes. But divorce is too destructive an evil to compromise with simply to keep peace in a preacher's family. People are counting on hearing truth from their pulpits.

It was the universal teaching of all Christians for nineteen centuries that all of these were serious sin: abortion, masturbation, and, under ordinary circumstances, divorce and remarriage. Any one of them was incompatible with the Christian life. Holding to historic Christian morality does not mean we cannot love the fallen sinner. In fact, we are all fallen sinners. That is all the more reason we should not tamper with the rules. Compromising on the truth helps no one, least of all those struggling against sin. The standards must not be lowered for our convenience.

Evangelicals as a whole do not even seem to be aware of the tremendous shift that Christianity in the twentieth

century has experienced on moral issues. The situation reminds me of something Thoreau once observed: You may
not have seen the milk being watered down, but if you see
a trout swimming in it, you have good cause to suspect
that it is so.

But even this problem within Evangelicalism was not
enough to convince me that the Catholic Church was right.
I believed that Catholics were fundamentally flawed in their
views on salvation, Mary, and eschatology. It seemed to be an
ironic twist that they were morally upright. Before I could
accept their moral teaching as a sign of God's hand, I had to
work through the theological and biblical questions.

After I had done that, my perspective necessarily changed.
Jesus said that you shall know the tree by its fruit: "By their
fruit you will recognize them. . . . A good tree cannot bear
bad fruit, and a bad tree cannot bear good fruit . . . by their
fruit you will recognize them" (Mt 7:16–20; see also Mt
12:33 and Lk 6:43–45). This teaching is true of the Catholic
Church. The Church as Church teaches a moral purity that is
truly unique in the world today.

All throughout her history, up to the present day, no other
church has had the numbers of people striving to live out
Christ's commands. Some, such as Augustine, came to the
Catholic faith from a heresy (Manicheaism). Others were
"cradle Catholics" who never left. Some have lived as Christians in religious communities. Some have lived in secular
surroundings. Even today there are some dozen Catholic orders that accept people in secular life as full members. (As an
Evangelical, I had been unaware of these orders.) In all these
cases, the tree has borne good fruit.

As an Evangelical, I was surprised when I found that the
Church sees her moral teaching as part of that initial truth
handed to her by the apostles for safeguarding. The moral

standards of the Catholic Church find their source in the original deposit of faith entrusted to the first bishops. That is why she will not budge in her moral teaching. Better to lose all of England to a schism, as in the time of King Henry VIII, than to be guilty of modifying Christ's commands concerning the sanctity of the marriage bond.

Nowhere is the refusal to modify rules for our convenience clearer than in the Catholic Church's teaching on birth control. Hers is virtually the only Christian voice still opposing artificial birth control. She knows she has no authority to tamper with the original deposit of the faith.

First we need to understand what the Church actually teaches. As the old country preacher said, "I know some people will feel that I've left preaching and gone to meddling, but here goes anyway."

Many Catholics dislike the term "birth control". They point out that its proponents support neither *birth* nor *control*. However, the historic Christian position is that responsible family planning is fine when it is the result of *self-control*. The size and spacing of a family can be controlled via natural family planning (NFP), which avoids artificial means. There is certainly nothing wrong with having only one or two children if that is really God's will and the parents are generously open to life. But NFP always leaves the possibility that God may create life on any given occasion. It does not impede the workings of God.

The important point is to be open to life's creation, if God willed it. Life is always better than non-life. Always. This view on the creation of life itself is why being prolife means much more to a Catholic than to an Evangelical. To an Evangelical, being prolife means being antiabortion. To a Catholic, it is much, much more. A Catholic can honestly say, "I love life!"

But perhaps we should start at the beginning. As with all moral questions, the discussion should start with our purpose for being here. What is the purpose of having children? This seems to be a question that too few Christians ask themselves today. Is it to fulfill my needs to be a parent? Is it to please the grandparents? Is it to have someone to control or to love?

The Catholic Church was the first place I found the answer to this question clearly taught with consistency. Evangelicals might agree with the answer, but rarely do they make the connection on their own. As with all of life, the purpose of children is *to bring praise and glory to God eternally*. God's glory underlies all moral behavior, including our sexual behavior. Here's the connection: *every* child we bring into the world *can glorify God* for *all eternity* in heaven. This adds to the glory God so richly deserves.

Some schools of economic theory stress that children do not consume wealth, they create it. Each new human adds to the material prosperity of the entire human family. (This principle directly contradicts the population-control crowd.) But what we do here is only the prelude to the main event, in eternity. Adding to our material prosperity pales in importance next to the privilege of adding to God's eternal glory.

Christian parents have the singularly important task of populating heaven with saints. Every life created by God in concert with a man and woman can live forever to bring eternal praise and glory to God in heaven. We help populate heaven with "praise-givers". If the angels of heaven rejoice when one sinner repents (Lk 15:10), what makes us think that heaven doesn't resound with praise when a new eternal soul comes into being?

Angels are ontologically different from humans. God alone made the angels. There is only a set number of them.

They cannot procreate. Heaven will never have more angels than it does now, unless God directly creates new ones. But when God made humans, he gave them the privilege of working in concert with him in creating new humans. What a privilege!

This freedom elevates Christian parenthood to its proper level. A mother does a high and holy thing when she gives birth. Her work in mothering even has salvific ramifications (1 Tim 2:15). A father feeds and clothes future saints of heaven when he provides for his family. He will be rewarded in heaven for providing for his family as a Christian should: "Whatever you did for one of the least of these . . . you did for me" (Mt 25:34–40, 1 Tim 5:7).

This is exactly what being a Christian is all about: putting God's eternal glory before our own desires. "To him [God] be the glory forever! . . . Therefore . . . offer your *bodies* as living sacrifices . . . this is your spiritual act of worship" (Rom 11:36–12:1). These verses point out that the offering of our bodies to God is directly related to his glory. God wants us to sacrifice our *bodies* for his service. That includes all of our bodies, even (dare I say, especially) our reproductive organs.

There is something innately "God-loving" about bringing a new life into being. That new life can love God forever. Never do we work more closely with God than in the marriage bed. But allowing God's will in this area requires generosity.

When Colleen and I started visiting various Catholic churches, we immediately noticed a dramatic difference in people's attitudes. At the time, we had six children ranging in age from two to thirteen. Catholics might not all obey the Church's teaching on birth control, but most respect those who do. We had a surprising number of people comment positively on the size of our family. One comment I will never forget was "My, I admire your generosity." I had never before thought of our family in those terms.

Evangelicals, on the other hand, treat large families in much the same manner as does the rest of American culture. Colleen and I joke about the "fundamentalist four". Many Evangelicals seem to think it is acceptable to have four or fewer children; but have more than four, and you will be criticized. We have been in stores when total strangers have approached us with, "Good heavens! These aren't all yours, are they?" When Colleen was pregnant with our sixth child, we had relatives and Evangelical friends who refused to congratulate us. We actually heard some lectures from some of them. One of the pastors at our Evangelical church insisted that he was going to drive me to the clinic for a vasectomy. I declined as graciously as I could.

When I tell Evangelicals about my family, their comments are generally predictable. First, they comment disparagingly about how much time and energy that many children must take. Our response is, "Yes, they do take time. But after the second one, the *additional* time each one takes is dramatically less." The second comment is usually "But that many children must be so expensive!" The honest response is, "Yes, they are. But the cost of six children is not triple the cost of two or six times the cost of one."

What lies behind these comments is bothersome. Both comments betray an underlying attitude of selfishness. One is a selfishness with time and energy, and the other, with money. With whom are we being selfish? It is with God himself. The reason he created the oneness of marriage was to give *himself* children to praise him. "Has not the Lord made husband and wife one? . . . And why one? Because he was seeking godly offspring" (Malachi 2:15). Our selfishness is tantamount to refusing God our assistance in enhancing his glory for all eternity.

Where did we get the idea that what is important is how many children *we* want? Or that we must provide for our children in a manner that makes our neighbors envious? Why do many Christians feel it is their duty to discourage others from having large families? Who first tried to convince us that children are a burden to be minimized? Must Christians accept the antichild philosophy of American culture? What about the eternal plans of God?

The Bible calls children a blessing: "Sons are a heritage from the Lord, children a reward from him" (Ps 127:3–5). This is in direct opposition to the views of those who extol the virtues of small families. Margaret Sanger, founder of the organization now known as Planned Parenthood, wrote (in her book *Women and the New Race*, p. 63): "The most merciful thing that the large family does to one of its infant members is to kill it."

A Christian knows he can never out-give God. It seems that the more generous we are with God, the more generous he is with us. However, there is nothing that will test a couple's generosity more than their willingness to bear children for God's eternal glory. The issue really boils down to one of generosity: generosity with God.

I have not always thought this way. When we first married, Colleen and I, like almost every other Evangelical couple we knew, used artificial birth control. I was only nominally prolife until about two years after leaving seminary. I wanted two or three children. It was only after I saw Colleen with our children that God opened my mind to the possibility of more. Watching her care for our children gave me a glimpse of God's charity in action. Colleen was always much closer to biblical teaching on this issue than was I. She saw children as a blessing and would never consider any permanent means of birth control.

I was still uneasy during one of her later pregnancies. I was beginning to think that maybe we did have too many children. Evangelical friends were openly criticizing us for the size of our family. I was worried about the financial commitments another child would bring, particularly regarding college tuition. At a crucial juncture in my thinking, the generosity of a Catholic friend helped my faith grow. She offered to share clothes with our family. She never criticized us for the size of our family or for our lack of faith. Being a good Catholic, she simply did something to help.

Although I did not talk much about it, God used that friend to teach me an important lesson. My lack of faith and charity was embarrassing. I was being selfish. After I became Catholic, my entire attitude toward children shifted. The turning point came when I agreed with God that the birth of another child would be an unmitigated blessing, even if I were fifty. I decided that being selfish with God was infinitely unwise. I am only forty-one, so this decision was an act of faith as momentous as any I have made.

The selfishness of artificial birth control has been labeled "onanism" since time immemorial. This word originated with the sin of Onan in Genesis 38:9–10. Yes, the Bible does discuss the use of artificial birth control. In Scripture, God deems its use worthy of death! Onan participated in the act of sex, a totally self-giving act, but, for selfish reasons, he artificially made conception impossible. God killed him for this one act of birth control. Certainly the fact that we now have more efficient scientific methods does not change the basic rightness or wrongness of the selfishness itself.

There is something innately selfish about wanting the pleasure of procreation without the responsibilities. Sex by its very nature is an act of total self-giving to one's partner. Dietrich von Hildebrand has described it as a relationship whose meaning is love and whose purpose is procreation. Artificial birth control allows one to go through the motions of unreservedly giving oneself without really giving anything at all. It makes the marriage act a lie.

I am, obviously, not discussing couples who have small families because of health conditions or through no fault of their own. Instead, I am referring to men and women who participate in sexual activity for what they can get rather than for what they can give. It is precisely this same selfish attitude that underlies all promiscuity. God's glory is not even a consideration to people who have this attitude.

God built humans with two basic drives. The hunger drive preserves my personal life. That is its primary purpose. I can enjoy it, but when I separate it from its purpose, I become guilty of gluttony. Gluttony is short-sighted. Its only consideration is the pleasure of the moment.

The sexual drive is the other basic drive. Its purpose is also to perpetuate life: the life of humanity. That is its primary purpose. I can enjoy it, but if I separate it from its purpose, I become guilty of the sexual sins. All sexual sins are short-sighted, also. They are a failure to appreciate the eternal perspective, which is the increase of God's glory.

When pleasure and purpose are totally severed, even homosexuality and masturbation can be made to sound sensible. We have stepped onto a slippery slope with no handrails.

This eternal perspective is the unifying moral perspective that links abortion, birth control, homosexuality, euthanasia, racism, masturbation, and divorce. It involves having a view to God's glory and how he made humanity. This leads us to a godly perspective on life—its creation, its dignity, its ultimate purpose, and its preservation.

Even from a strictly legal standpoint, this unity of the issues is evident. *Roe v. Wade* (1973) was the court case that in effect legalized abortion in the United States. Legal experts have argued that this decision would have been impossible without the foundation that had been laid in an earlier case, *Griswold v. Connecticut* (1965). Few Evangelicals seem to have heard of this case. In it, the Supreme Court struck down any state law that prohibited artificial means of birth control. (Evangelicals seem to forget that birth control within marriage was unlawful in the United States until just before the "sexual revolution".) This right to use artificial means of birth control was based on the "right to privacy". Eight years later, that "right to privacy" was expanded—to allow a woman to abort her child.

The legalization of birth control laid the foundation for the legalization of abortion. Evangelicals are now pointing out that the acceptance of abortion is leading to euthanasia and assisted suicide. Until the 1930s, *all* Christians of *all* theological persuasions agreed, along with Islam and Orthodox Judaism, that the uncrossable line in sexual sin was the use of artificial methods of birth control. Once that issue is separated from the rest, we can be conquered on any one of them. We have already seen the evidence. We have compromised on the underlying foundation of all these issues.

If we must draw a line, why not stick with historic Christianity? Evangelicals profess a desire to preserve original Christianity. I believe they are sincere in that profession. William F. Buckley once wrote that a person who is deciding to be a conservative must determine what it is he wishes to preserve. For example, a political conservative in Russia is a person who wishes to preserve the Old Soviet Union and communism. In American politics, a conservative generally wishes to preserve the original intent of the Constitution. In Christianity, the Catholic bishop wishes to conserve the original teaching (including moral teaching) of the apostles. If we call ourselves Christians, we should wish to preserve the original Christian morality.

The fact that this teaching of the Church on birth control is unpopular bothers Evangelicals immensely. They are sure that its general unpopularity within the Church will lead to a modification in the teaching Magisterium of the Catholic Church. Nothing could be more naïve. The Church has been around for a long time. In fact, the Church is the oldest Western institution of any kind still in existence.

The Church remembers that at the Council of Nicaea (A.D. 324), Arianism was condemned. Evangelicals agree wholeheartedly with that Council because it clearly defined and proclaimed Christ's divinity. As we noted previously, however, for many years after that Council, there were more Arian heretics than there had been before the Council. The Church's proclamation of the truth had solidified the opposition.

Much the same thing can be expected with the moral teachings of the Church. From time to time, the proclamation of the truth will solidify the opposition. The victory of God's way over man's way will appear to be in peril. Even some Christians will not agree to put God's glory first. Human dignity will suffer. But Jesus promised that even the gates of hell would not prevail against the Church that he would build upon Peter. The teaching authority of the Church will not be compromised. She will always preserve the truth handed down from those original twelve men who turned the world on its head.

It may not make much difference in the broad scope of things, but "as for me and my household, we will serve the Lord" in his Church: one, holy, catholic, and apostolic (see Jos 24:15).

Epilogue

As this book was going to press, our three-year-old daughter experienced God's answer to prayer. She had been praying for a specific request for several months. At first, we thought she would soon forget about it, and so we did nothing. After a week, however, we saw that she was very serious. Colleen told her that although God hears all our prayers, he sometimes does not answer with a "yes". Her response was, "Well, then, I will just pray louder. If God hears my prayer, I know he will say 'yes'." That night, she virtually shouted her prayers.

The next night she declared that she wanted to go to church to pray. She was sure that God would hear her prayer and answer "yes" if she prayed there.

As parents, we have learned again that God does answer the sincere prayers of little three-year-old girls. We had believed it might not be possible, but Colleen is expecting our seventh child. The miracle of a new life is always so amazing, and our whole family is very excited about it. We feel truly blessed.

APPENDIX

Further Reading

If you are interested in further reading, there are at least two good ways to proceed. One is to look for authors who are helpful and to read anything you can find that they have written. I do that with some authors. There are several good ones with whom Evangelicals can start.

Warren H. Carroll has the best book series on Church history I have ever seen. It reads like a mystery. He starts with Adam and Eve and marches through history from there. The first book in the series is *The Founding of Christendom*. Carroll is a convert to Catholicism.

Scott and Kimberly Hahn have recorded some excellent talks. One of Scott's talks initiated my thinking on the Eucharist. I particularly enjoyed *Common Objections to the Catholic Faith*. Anything by either one of them is well worth the time. The Hahns both came to Catholicism from evangelicalism.

Tom Howard has written an excellent book detailing his own journey from evangelicalism to Catholicism—*Evangelical Is Not Enough*. He has several other excellent books in print, as well.

Karl Keating has written a wonderful book, *Catholicism and Fundamentalism*, which answers the charges of fundamentalists from a Catholic perspective. Although written for

Catholics, his book helped me put some issues to rest in my own pilgrimage.

Peter Kreeft has written excellent books on morality and philosophy. He also came to Catholicism from evangelicalism.

Father Mitchell Pacwa, S.J., is an Old Testament scholar who has made an excellent recorded presentation on the Eucharist. He is also an expert on the New Age movement.

Patrick Madrid has compiled the stories of eleven converts to Catholicism into a fine book, *Surprised by Truth*. Reading it is akin to attending an Evangelical "testimony time".

It should not need to be said, but the popes are a rich source for Evangelicals who want to read more about the Catholic faith. Anything written by Pope John Paul II is a good place to start, but don't be afraid to reach back into history and read the encyclicals (short topical teachings) of earlier popes. Every Evangelical would do well to read *Humanae vitae* (Pope Paul VI).

Along with the writings of the popes, you should look into the documents of the councils of the Church. I thought reading them would be similar to reading the minutes of the local Evangelical church's annual meeting—boring. Nothing could be farther from the truth. They are peppered with Scripture. They are beautiful examples of a rich spirituality in the Catholic Church's leadership. They have an added advantage as well: they are authoritative.

The other group of authors whom Evangelicals should read, but rarely do, is the early Fathers of the Church. All the extant Christian writings from the first three hundred years of the Church can be shelved on one bookshelf. That amount of literature is not too overwhelming. An excellent place to start is the *Patrology* series edited by Johannes Quasten.

Fulfilling the desires of Vatican II, the Church has just

published the *Catechism of the Catholic Church*. Anyone who wants to know what Catholics believe about a topic should buy the *Catechism*. It is well indexed and very readable. Already a worldwide best seller, it is the first universal catechism published in about half a millennium. It has the authority of the Church as Church behind it.

The second method of approach when starting to research Catholicism is through Catholic publishing houses and bookstores. They can usually recommend a book on a particular topic. I will mention only a few publishers I have found most helpful to me:

Catholic Answers:
> —ORDERS, P. O. Box 199000, San Diego, CA 92159.
> —OTHER CORRESPONDENCE, 2020 Gillespie Way, El Cajon, CA 93020; TEL 888–291–8000; www.catholic.com.

Catholics United for the Faith, 827 N. Fourth St., Steubenville, OH 43952; TEL 800–693–2484; www.cuf.org.

Christendom Press, 134 Christendom Drive, Front Royal, VA 22630; TEL 800–698–6649; www.christendompress.com.

Daughters of St. Paul, 50 St. Paul's Ave., Boston, MA 02130 (they have bookstores in various cities in the United States); TEL 800–836–9723; www.pauline.org.

Ignatius Press, P.O. Box 1339, Fort Collins, CO 80522; TEL 800–651–1531; www.ignatius.com.

Our Sunday Visitor, 200 Noll Plaza, Huntington, IN 46750; TEL 800–348–2440; www.oursundayvisitor.com.

St. Joseph Communicatons, P.O. Box 1991, Suite 83, Tehachapi, CA 93581; www.saintjoe.com.